GOOD JOB, BRAIN!

TRIVIA, QUIZZES, AND MORE FUN

from

THE POPULAR
PUB QUIZ PODCAST

D1535668

KAREN CHU ✳ COLIN FELTON ✳ DANA NELSON ✳ CHRIS KOHLER

Ulysses Press

Published in the United States by
ULYSSES PRESS
P.O. Box 3440
Berkeley, CA 94703
www.ulyssespress.com

ISBN: 978-1-61243-600-5
Library of Congress Control Number 2016934492

Printed in the United States by United Graphics Inc.

10 9 8 7 6 5 4 3 2 1

Acquisitions Editor: Casie Vogel
Managing Editor: Claire Chun
Project Editor: Caety Klingman
Editor: Phyllis Elving
Proofreader: Kate St.Clair
Layout: Jake Flaherty

Distributed by Publishers Group West

CONTENTS

Introduction   1

Preface   2

Foreword   3

Author's Note   4

Pop Culture 4-Ever   **5**

Bored of Board Games   6

William Fake-Speare   9

Call Me a Doctor   11

Movies Go to the Movies!   13

WhatIsThisDotCom.com   15

What Would Keanu Do?   18

Sidekicks   22

Who's on First?   25

Lifetime Movie or Not Lifetime Movie?   28

Sequel-ize Me   31

The Perfect Band Name   33

Beep Me Maybe   36

Getting That Last Word In   39

Remember These Movie Quotes?   41

William Shake-Yo'-Booty-Speare   43

A Number of Problems   45

Wilderness Girls   46

Fun Time Vocab Corner   49

TV Rebus Time!   50

1992 at the Movies!   55

Weird Science, Weirder Animals   59

Celebritaxonomy   60

A Very Average Human Body by the Numbers   62

The Big Five   65

The Flying Tailor   66

Animal Secretion Spotlight: Bombardier Beetle   68

Scarce Hairs   69

One Hump or Two?   71

Time Flies Like an Arrow; Urinal Flies Like Pee   72

Christmas with Bugs   73

Spy Cat!   75

Extreme Animals   77

Mighty Menacing Mercury   80

Animal Secretion Spotlight: Bedtime Booger Bubble   82

Tush Trivia   83

Nobel's Safety Powder   86

So It's Come to This: A Page about Boogers   88

(Mostly) Cute Baby Animals   89

Like an Animal! 91

The Centaur of Attention 93

Who, What, and Where 95

Official State Whatevers 96

Brad Pitt or Lasers? 99

Setting Sail On the Garbage Ship 101

Belgium or Not Belgium? 103

Sounds Like a Capital Idea! 105

Butt Is It Art? 107

License to Quiz 109

Brad Pitt or Lasers? Part II 111

OMGeography! 113

Provinces, Eh? 116

Catch of the Day 118

The Truth About Buried Treasure 122

Vexing Vexillology 124

Money Makes the World Go 'Round 127

Um, Actually... 129

Japan or Not Japan? 133

Brad Pitt or Lasers? Part III 135

Angels and Devils 137

Common Thread 140

Stuff Yo' Face

Stuff Yo' Face   **145**

The Other Toroidal Breakfast   146

Cocktail!   148

Fraudulent Foods and Flavor Foolers   152

Your Medicine Is Like Bad Love   154

Diner Lingo   156

Would You Care for a Bowl of Worms?   159

Hey, Where'd You Get That Cheese?   161

Animal Secretion Spotlight: Beaver Butt Juice   164

Truth in Advertising   166

Um, Actually: Food Edition   169

A Balthazar for the Table, Please!   172

Word Nerdery   **175**

Hey, Let's Actually Use Latin Correctly!   176

Back Talk   178

Who, What, or Where?   181

Our Favorite Eggcorns   184

Mind Cruncher   186

I Forgot What I Was Supposed to Remember   189

I Mustache You a Question: The *Good Job, Brain!* Crossword   191

Fortune-Telling for Dummies   196

Interlopers   199

One Letter Off   201

Japanese Words You Already Know   203

B-R-A-I-N Q-U-I-Z   205

On Your Marks   207

My Polish Nail Polish   210

Word Swap   214

Fancy Pants   217

Pardon My French   219

Who, What, or Where? Part II   221

Remembering the Bill of Rights   224

The *Good Job, Brain!* Cryptic Crossword   226

Guide to Solving Cryptics   229

The *Good Job, Brain!* Guide to How to Pub-Quiz Gooder 239

Good Job, Brain! Thanks   246

About Good Job, Brain!   248

About the Authors   248

INTRODUCTION

 **BY KAREN**

We've been playing pub trivia since 2008. Every single week.

Despite our collective life events of changing jobs, moving to new digs, getting married, having babies, traveling for work, dealing with emergencies, and basically tackling whatever life throws at us, we still manage to carve time for pub trivia.

Every. Single. Week.

What is so alluring about pub trivia that it keeps us coming back for more? Well, we have a theory. As adults, it's rare to find activities that allow you and your friends to work together outside of professional and school environments. When was the last time you and your friends cooperated and accomplished something for fun? We think this may be the reason people play pickup basketball, team together for a game of *League of Legends*, or meet up at a bar and answer quiz questions for three hours.

There's an element of joy in trivia. And that joy doesn't necessarily come from being right, or being a poindexter know-it-all. I believe the real joy in trivia comes from learning something cool and getting to the point where you basically *cannot wait* to share it with others. The four of us are just so fortunate to have found each other. And we knew there were other people out there who were as obsessively curious as we are, who find joy in learning that you can use Cheez Whiz as shaving cream, that Captain Crunch's full name is Horatio Magellan Crunch, and that Youppi! (whose face looks like an upside-down uterus) is the first mascot to transfer from one major sports franchise to another.

This is why we started the *Good Job, Brain!* podcast. We wanted to invite the whole world to join our pub trivia table, and to revel in all the weird facts around us. And this book you're holding—this is us, too, sharing our joy with you. So what are you waiting for? Flip the page and let's be curious together.

PREFACE

BY CHRIS

One Thursday in 2008, Karen and I stopped at a local chain pub, Elephant & Castle, to grab dinner. We sat down at our table to find that we had walked into the middle of a night of pub trivia, and the host was reading out the answers to the previous round in a charming British accent.

"Chris," Karen said, "I know you really want to eat here, but if we can't play along with this trivia, we have to leave." Karen couldn't sit there and listen to trivia questions without being able to play along. Fortunately, they gave us an answer booklet and let us join in while the quiz was in progress. (Good thing, because I was hungry.) We wrote down "Baby Dog Time" as our team name, after what we called it when we picked up Karen's giant pit bull Otis and cradled him like a baby. We lost that round of trivia, of course, and we lost the next week, and the week after that. And we lost a lot thereafter. But soon something crazy started happening. We kept losing, but by less of a margin each time.

Eventually we started winning, and a few years later Karen had the bright idea of turning our weekly trivia nights into a podcast, only this time we'd call it something a little less esoteric than "Baby Dog Time." What you're about to read are some of our favorite segments, quizzes, and puzzles from four years of the *Good Job, Brain!* podcast, plus some new stuff we came up with just for you. If you're a longtime *GJB* listener, thanks for all your support over the years—it has helped us put this book together! If you're just joining the *GJB* family for the first time, we hope you enjoy this journey into our weird obsessions.

FOREWORD

While other book-minded kids were getting lost in the pages of *The Hobbit* or *A Wrinkle in Time*, I was busy with *The Big Book of Amazing Facts*, a massive (to my young eyes) collection of trivia and campy illustrations. I got it as a present for Christmas when I was eight, and I don't think I put it down until sometime the following spring. My love affair with trivia books had begun.

The only downside to my obsession with trivia collections was that unless something happened to show up on a test at school, the payoff was rather slim. So you can imagine my sheer and utter delight when I discovered the board game Trivial Pursuit a few years later. Not only could I put my heretofore-useless knowledge to use, but I could also use it in a "team sport." By the time I got to college and discovered the magic of the pub quiz—Beer! Trivia! Together!—I decided I'd found my calling in life: shouting out answers and hoping to be right.

I'm so lucky to have met Karen, Dana, and Chris. We've been playing pub quizzes together longer than any job I've had, and creating the *Good Job, Brain!* podcast with them has been one of the most rewarding things I've ever done. It's such a joy for us to get together each week and quiz it up with other teams at the pub, or to crowd around our table gabbing into our microphones as we record our show. And now it's come full circle for me. If this book full of facts, quizzes, and outright weirdness can convey even a small fraction of the love we have for trivia, then we've done our jobs. Enjoy!

AUTHOR'S NOTE

 **BY DANA**

This book is a great reflection of what we find interesting in trivia, both as a pub team and as a podcast. There's an entire chapter on food, for example. We almost named the science chapter "Gross Stuff," but decided that not all the stories are gross (just most of them).

You'll find *Good Job, Brain!* podcast favorites such as "William Shakespeare Goes to a House Party," "Brad Pitt or Lasers," and "Belgium or Not Belgium." We've also included plenty of new stuff, like a Keanu Reeves–themed connect-the-dots puzzle, TV-show rebuses, and a really cool story about a fish with a runny nose.

On the podcast, we challenge each other. With this book, we get a chance to challenge you, our dear brainy reader. As you try your hand at these quizzes, be sure to check out the answer sections to dig even deeper.

We hope you find this book as enjoyable to read as it was to write.

 SO WHAT ARE YOU WAITING FOR?
FLIP THE PAGE—AND LET'S BE CURIOUS TOGETHER.

POP CULTURE 4-EVER

CELEBRITIES, MOVIES, TV, MUSIC, MORE.

BINGEING ON EPISODES OF *FRIENDS* IS TOTALLY ACCEPTABLE IF IT HELPS YOU WIN A PUB QUIZ!

BORED OF BOARD GAMES

BY CHRIS

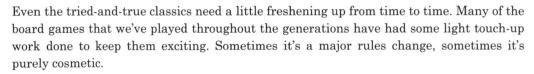

Even the tried-and-true classics need a little freshening up from time to time. Many of the board games that we've played throughout the generations have had some light touch-up work done to keep them exciting. Sometimes it's a major rules change, sometimes it's purely cosmetic.

Write the letter corresponding to the classic board game into the blank next to the rule alteration it once went through. As a bonus, look around before you check your answers and you may find a 13th classic board game hiding somewhere on the page.

RULE ALTERATION

1. ____ Added a penalty for unsuccessful challenge.

2. ____ Pawns reduced from four to three per player.

3. ____ Added a "Wild Card" category.

4. ____ "Gloppy the Molasses Monster" renamed "Gloppy the Chocolate Monster."

5. ____ Added "Brain Freeze."

6. ____ Triangles and stars changed to Roman numerals, and back again.

7. ____ Dark purple changed to brown.

8. ____ Called "Frustration!" in the U.K.

9. ____ Character renamed "Dr. Black."

10. ____ Removed snakes.

11. ____ Loosened the "Joker" rule.

12. ____ Renamed from "The Captain's Mistress."

GOOD JOB, **BRAIN!**

BOARD GAME

A. Operation

B. Chutes and Ladders

C. Trivial Pursuit

D. Connect Four

E. Clue

F. Trouble

G. Sorry!

H. Candy Land

I. Monopoly

J. Scrabble

K. Yahtzee

L. Risk

Once you've written in your answers, read down the column of letters to find the hidden board game: LIFE.

1. **J.** Scrabble (Penalty added for unsuccessful challenge.)

2. **G.** Sorry! (Pawns reduced from four to three per player.)

3. **C.** Trivial Pursuit (Added a "Wild Card" category.)

4. **H.** Candy Land ("Gloppy the Molasses Monster" renamed "Gloppy the Chocolate Monster.")

5. **A.** Operation (Added "Brain Freeze.")

6. **L.** Risk (Triangles and stars changed to Roman numerals, and back again.)

7. **I.** Monopoly (Dark purple changed to brown.)

8. **F.** Trouble (Called "Frustration!" in the U.K.)

9. **E.** Clue (Character renamed "Dr. Black.")

10. **B.** Chutes and Ladders (Removed snakes.)

11. **K.** Yahtzee (Loosened the "Joker" rule.)

12. **D.** Connect Four (Renamed from "The Captain's Mistress.")

WILLIAM FAKE-SPEARE

BY KAREN

Get yo' hands up and yo' collars frilled, because history's favorite Bizz-ard is storming into this house party all the way from Stratford-Up-On-Yo'-Avon! The Elizabethan lyrics below are all rewritten versions of well-known lines from famous party songs. Can you figure out which dance jams Willy Fake is rocking on the microphone?

LYRICS

1. *I wilt ne'er relinquish thee, nor causeth thee dismay;*
   Nor divert, or forsaketh thee.

2. *'Tis mad, yet: give me leave, pray, to present*
   Mine numerals, and perhaps convene anon.

3. *Allow hoofs to be fancy-free, and wand'ring—*
   Remove thine mules, donned on the Lord's Day.

4. *From the lad of alabaster visage, do I*
   Summon a performance of song, eccentric.

5. *Naught any betrothed maidens! Naught any betrothed maidens:*
   I wouldst you presently, uplift your palms.

6. *Halt! Rally to me, and hark:*
   I, the frosted knave, hath returned, now with modish forging.

7. *What gamester hath emancipated mine*
   Hounds? What gamester, what gamester—what gamester?

1. *Never gonna give you up. Never gonna let you down. Never gonna run around, and desert you.*

   "Never Gonna Give You Up" by Rick Astley

2. *And this is crazy. Here's my number. Call me maybe.*

   "Call Me Maybe" by Carly Rae Jepsen

3. *Footloose. Kick off your Sunday shoes.*

   "Footloose" by Kenny Loggins

4. *Play that funky music, white boy.*

   "Play That Funky Music" by Wild Cherry

5. *All the single ladies, all the single ladies. Put your hands up!*

   "Single Ladies" by Beyoncé

6. *Stop, collaborate, and listen. Ice is back with my brand new invention.*

   "Ice, Ice, Baby" by Vanilla Ice

7. *Who let the dogs out? Who? Who? Who?*

   "Who Let the Dogs Out" by Baha Men

CALL ME A DOCTOR

BY COLIN

I'm not a doctor, nor do I play one on TV. So for this quiz I'm adopting the personas of several famous people (real and fictional) who go by "Doctor" or "Doc." For each question I'll provide a few hints to my identity, and you tell me who I am!

CLUES

1. I was a doctor in the German army. I injured my ankle during a ski trip in 1945, and when I realized how harsh my standard issue army boots were, I invented more therapeutic footwear. Who am I?

Colin, I actually do have this rash I'm hoping you can take a quick look-see at.

CHRIS

2. My real name is Julius Winfield Erving II, but I picked up some nicknames on the basketball court in the '60s and '70s, including "Houdini" and "Black Moses. Who am I?

3. I'm the title character in a Nobel Prize–winning 1957 novel that was famously banned in the Soviet Union. Who am I?

4. After being busted for drinking in my dorm room during Prohibition, I was kicked off the staff of my college humor magazine. In order to continue submitting cartoons, I adopted a variety of pen names, including my now-famous middle name. Who am I?

5. As a young woman in the 1940s, I was trained as an Israeli military sniper. But these days I'm better known for my work bringing people together…intimately. Who am I?

6. I was trained as a dentist in Philadelphia before moving west in the 1870s and becoming a professional gambler. I then fell in with a bad crowd in Arizona. Who am I?

7. If you've been in a Jewish deli in the last 100 years, you've probably seen the legacy of my creation: a digestive tonic made primarily of celery seed and sugar. Who am I?

8. I earned my affectionate nickname as a physician in the 1940s, fighting contagious disease among Haiti's poor. But ultimately I became a feared dictator. Who am I?

1. **Doc Martens**. (My full name is Dr. Klaus Martens.)

2. **Dr. J**.

3. **Doctor Zhivago**, from the novel by Boris Pasternak.

4. **Dr. Seuss**. (My real name is Theodor Seuss Geisel.)

5. **Dr. Ruth Westheimer**. (Yes, I was actually trained as a sniper! Luckily, I never shot anyone.)

6. **Doc Holliday**. (My full name is John Henry Holliday.)

7. **Dr. Brown**, "inventor" of Dr. Brown's Cel-Ray soda. (Sadly, I am most likely a fictional creation for marketing purposes.)

8. **François "Papa Doc" Duvalier**.

MOVIES GO TO THE MOVIES!

BY CHRIS

We love the movies, and so do the movies. The following is a list of films you may be familiar with, even though they don't, technically, exist. These are fictitious movies within actual films. Sometimes they were just referred to by title, and sometimes we even saw "clips" from these films. Think you can tell me the real movies in which these fake movies played a role?

FICTITIOUS FILMS

1. *Simple Jack*

2. *Good Will Hunting 2: Hunting Season*

3. *Jews in Space*

4. *Ass*

5. *Angels with Filthy Souls*

6. *Angels with Even Filthier Souls*

7. *Don't*

8. *Gandhi II*

9. *Nation's Pride*

10. *Asses of Fire*

11. *Turbo Man*

12. *Jaws 19*

13. *Rocky 5000*

14. *The Dancing Cavalier*

15. *Brock Landers: Angels Live in My Town*

16. *Logjammin'*

1. *Tropic Thunder*

2. *Jay and Silent Bob Strike Back*

3. *History of the World, Part I*

4. *Idiocracy*

5. *Home Alone*

6. *Home Alone 2: Lost in New York*

7. *Grindhouse*

8. *UHF*

9. *Inglourious Basterds*

10. *South Park: Bigger, Longer, and Uncut*

11. *Jingle All the Way*

12. *Back to the Future Part II*

13. *Spaceballs*

14. *Singin' in the Rain*

15. *Boogie Nights*

16. *The Big Lebowski*

WHATISTHISDOTCOM.COM

BY DANA

During the dot-com bubble of the late 1990s and early 2000s, it seemed like all anyone needed for a million-dollar investment was a quirky domain name and a wisp of a business idea. Some of the companies flourished—Amazon, for instance—but many shut down immediately after their launch parties. The companies in this quiz are in the second category. Based on the names, can you guess what service they provided?

QUESTIONS

1. Beenz.com
   a. Online currency
   b. Food delivery
   c. Heart-health supplements

2. Boo.com
   a. Halloween costume clearinghouse
   b. Clothing
   c. Matchmaking service

3. Flooz.com
   a. Social network
   b. Flight-booking service
   c. Online currency

4. Kibu.com
   a. Pet supplies
   b. Community site for teen girls
   c. Custom Japanese erasers and stationery

5. Kozmo.com
   a. Community site for women
   b. Horoscope site
   c. Home delivery service

6. Pixelon.com
   a. Custom server support
   b. Chat service
   c. Internet video streaming

7. Pop.com
   a. Movie streaming
   b. Music review site
   c. Fresh, buttery popcorn delivery service

8. Pseudo.com
   a. Webcasting
   b. Men's suits
   c. Precursor to *Wikipedia*

1. **(a) Online currency**. Beenz.com (as in "beans" as slang for money) was an online currency company that launched in 1998. Basically, you earned beenz by shopping and browsing around the Internet, and beenz were redeemable for items from certain stores. It's reported that Beenz.com raised almost $100 million from investors. It shut down in 2001.

2. **(b) Clothing**. Boo.com was a British online clothing retailer. Founded in 1998, it went through $135 million in venture capital in 18 months before shutting down in 2000.

3. **(c) Online currency**. Flooz.com was an online currency company, similar to Beenz.com. The word "Flooz" is based on *fuloos*, an Arabic word for money. In 2001, the FBI informed Flooz that a Russian crime syndicate was using Flooz to launder money from stolen credit card numbers. Whether or not this was related to its closure, Flooz shut down in August 2001.

4. **(b) Community site for teen girls**. Kibu.com was a community site for teen girls, launched in 2000. It had a $1 million launch party and shut down 46 days later.

5. **(c) Home delivery service**. Kozmo.com launched in 1998 as a home delivery service that guaranteed deliveries in an hour. It raised $280 million and at its height was offered in nine cities. The business model of no minimum purchase and free delivery proved unsustainable, and the company shut down in 2001.

6. **(c) Internet video streaming**. Pixelon.com was an early Internet video streaming service founded in 1998. It raised around $35 million in early investments and spent $16 million of it on "iBASH '99," a celebrity-filled launch party in Las Vegas. This party featured a number of big-name musical acts, including a reunion performance by The Who. The launch party was to be streamed live on the Web using Pixelon—but the service didn't work. It turned out that the technology had been misrepresented to investors and that its

founder—who'd been living under an assumed name—had been convicted of stock fraud in Virginia and was on that state's most-wanted list. Pixelon folded soon after this information came out.

7. **(a) Movie streaming**. Pop.com was a film distribution company backed by Steven Spielberg, Ron Howard, and Jeffrey Katzenberg, with funding from Paul Allen. The idea was that Hollywood studios and celebrities would create animated and live-action content especially for the site. Pop.com was announced in late 1999, millions of dollars were spent on it, and it shut down in 2000 without ever being launched.

8. **(a) Webcasting**. Pseudo.com was an audio and video webcasting site started in 1993 and shut down in 2000. The site's founder estimated that over the course of its life, Pseudo.com burned through $25 million in investment money. He also confessed in 2008 that the entire project was a "fake company" and a "long form piece of conceptual art."

WHAT WOULD KEANU DO?

BY DANA

I have seen nearly all the movies on International Superstar™ Keanu Reeves's IMDb page at least once (very cool achievement, I know). In an attempt to put my dedication to his prodigious *oeuvre* to use, I've constructed this quiz about Keanu movies. Your job is to match each title with the profession of Keanu's character in that movie. Use your answers to connect the dots in the correct order to reveal a Keanu-riffic surprise.

For example, the first movie on the list is *Bill and Ted's Bogus Journey*, in which he plays a Rocker (*S* on the list of professions), so *S* is the starting dot in the puzzle. Good luck!

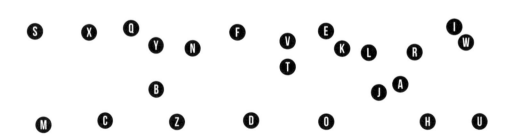

GOOD JOB, **BRAIN!**

MOVIES

1. ____ *Bill & Ted's Bogus Journey*
2. ____ *Bill & Ted's Excellent Adventure*
3. ____ *Bram Stoker's Dracula*
4. ____ *Chain Reaction*
5. ____ *Constantine*
6. ____ *Dangerous Liaisons*
7. ____ *The Day the Earth Stood Still*
8. ____ *The Devil's Advocate*
9. ____ *Hardball*
10. ____ *Henry's Crime*
11. ____ *John Wick*
12. ____ *Johnny Mnemonic*
13. ____ *The Lake House*
14. ____ *Little Buddha*
15. ____ *The Matrix*
16. ____ *Much Ado About Nothing*
17. ____ *My Own Private Idaho*
18. ____ *Point Break*
19. ____ *The Replacements*
20. ____ *Something's Gotta Give*
21. ____ *Speed*
22. ____ *Street Kings*
23. ____ *Sweet November*
24. ____ *Thumbsucker*
25. ____ *A Walk in the Clouds*
26. ____ *The Watcher*

PROFESSIONS

A. Ad executive
B. Alien messenger
C. Alternative energy researcher
D. Architect
E. Computer programmer
F. Courier
G. Defense attorney
H. Dentist
I. Detective
J. Doctor
K. FBI agent
L. Football player
M. High school student
N. Hit man
O. Hustler
P. Inner-city baseball coach
Q. Music teacher
R. Police officer
S. Rocker
T. Royal bastard
U. Serial killer
V. Siddhartha
W. Soldier
X. Solicitor
Y. Supernatural detective
Z. Toll collector

1. **S.** Rocker (*Bill and Ted's Bogus Journey*)

2. **M.** High school student (*Bill and Ted's Excellent Adventure*)

3. **X.** Solicitor (*Bram Stoker's Dracula*)

4. **C.** Alternative energy researcher (*Chain Reaction*)

5. **Y.** Supernatural detective (*Constantine*)

6. **Q.** Music teacher (*Dangerous Liaisons*)

7. **B.** Alien messenger (*The Day the Earth Stood Still*)

8. **G.** Defense attorney (*The Devil's Advocate*)

9. **P.** Inner-city baseball coach (*Hardball*)

10. **Z.** Toll collector (*Henry's Crime*)

11. **N.** Hit man (*John Wick*)

12. **F.** Courier (*Johnny Mnemonic*)

13. **D.** Architect (*The Lake House*)

14. **V.** Siddhartha (*Little Buddha*)

15. **E.** Computer programmer (*The Matrix*)

16. **T.** Royal bastard (*Much Ado About Nothing*)

17. **O.** Hustler (*My Own Private Idaho*)

18. **K.** FBI agent (*Point Break*)

19. **L.** Football player (*The Replacements*)

20. **J.** Doctor (*Something's Gotta Give*)

What I find most impressive is that Keanu performed all 26 of these roles using only three facial expressions.

COLIN

I believe you mean, "three AMAZING facial expressions."

DANA

21. R. Police officer (*Speed*)

22. I. Detective (*Street Kings*)

23. A. Ad executive (*Sweet November*)

24. H. Dentist (*Thumbsucker*)

25. W. Soldier (*A Walk in the Clouds*)

26. U. Serial killer (*The Watcher*)

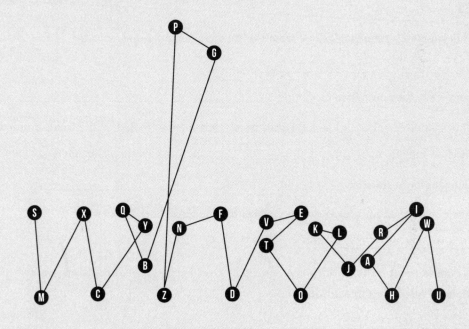

Whoa.

SIDEKICKS

BY CHRIS

Everybody needs a good sidekick, even if they're not superheroes. Here's a quiz about some well-known sidekicks. Write the answers in the grid provided, and the letters that land in the squares will spell the name of an actor from a movie appropriate to the theme of this quiz. Find the final answer by entering the (fictional) first name of his sidekick in the film.

CLUES

1. This sidekick's name is derived from the Russian word for dog, *sobaka*:

   ☐ ___ ___ ___ ___ ___ ___ ___

2. Lucy's sidekick on *I Love Lucy*: ___ ___ ☐ ___ ___ ___ ___ ___ ___ ___

3. This animated sidekick has a Swahili name that means "foolish, silly, weak-minded, careless, negligent": ___ ☐ ___ ___ ___ ___

4. Don Quixote's sidekick: ___ ___ ___ ☐ ___ ___ ___ ___ ___ ___ ___

5. After he ditched his sidekick role, he became the superhero Nightwing:

   ___ ___ ___ ☐ ___ ___ ___ ___ ___ ___ ___

6. A certain great sci-fi sidekick was played by this actor, whose initials are the two highest-value Scrabble letters:

   ___ ___ ___ ___ ___ ___ ___ ___ ___ ☐ ___ ___

7. Tom Hanks's sidekick in *Castaway* was a really good listener, but did little else:

   ___ ___ ___ ___ ☐ ___

8. This sidekick's most famous line is probably "Cover your heart!":

   ___ ___ ___ ___ ___ ⬜ ___ ___ ___ ___

9. Harry Potter's (male) sidekick: ⬜ ___ ___

10. The full first and last name of Frodo's sidekick:

    ___ ___ ___ ⬜ ___ ___ ___   ___ ___ ___ ___ ___ ___

11. John H. Watson is the sidekick of Sherlock Holmes; whose sidekick is Dr. David

    Q. Dawson? ___ ___ ⬜ ___ ___

FINAL ANSWER

Actor: ___ ___ ___ ___ ___   ___ ___ ___ ___ ___ ___

Sidekick: ___ ___ ___ ___ ___

1. <u>C</u>HEWBACCA

2. ET<u>H</u>EL MERTZ

3. P<u>U</u>MBAA, from *The Lion King*

4. SAN<u>C</u>HO PANZA

5. DIC<u>K</u> GRAYSON

6. ZACHARY QUI<u>N</u>TO, who played Spock in the *Star Trek* reboot

7. WILS<u>O</u>N (he was a volleyball)

8. SHORT <u>R</u>OUND, from *Indiana Jones and the Temple of Doom*

9. <u>R</u>ON

10. SAMW<u>I</u>SE GAMGEE

11. BA<u>S</u>IL, the Great Mouse Detective

FINAL ANSWER: Reading down the squares in the grid, you'll find CHUCK NORRIS, who starred in the classic film *Sidekicks* (of course) with Jonathan Brandis, who played BARRY.

The Chewbacca/dog connection doesn't end with the name. Han Solo's furry companion was directly inspired by George Lucas's dog, Indiana, who rode around with the *Star Wars* creator in the front seat of his car. (And a few years later, was also the source of Indiana Jones's name!)

COLIN

WHO'S ON FIRST?

BY COLIN

I've got some issues I need to deal with. They're collectible, slightly faded, and have that "old paper" smell. Don't worry, I'm not talking about my feelings—I'm talking about famous publications. This quiz is all about the people (and characters) who appeared on the covers of famous first issues! So hop in the Wayback Machine with me and we'll find out if you've got this covered.

CLUES

1. The debut issue of *Playboy* magazine from December 1953 featured this Hollywood sex symbol on its cover (and even more of her in the centerfold).

2. This rock musician, famous both as a solo artist and as part of an influential group, graced the cover of the premier issue of *Rolling Stone* magazine in November 1967.

3. The first issue of *TV Guide*, from April 1953, featured this (very) young person, the son of a famous Hollywood couple.

4. Name any three of the five Marvel Comics superheroes depicted on the cover of *The Avengers* #1, from September 1963.

5. In 1927, *Time* magazine featured this record-setting American for its first "Man of the Year" issue.

6. DC Comics legend Wonder Woman appeared on the cover of what magazine's first full issue in July 1972?

7. What is the primary claim to fame of model Babette March?

8. What is the name of the monocled, top hat–wearing dandy depicted on the cover of the first issue of *The New Yorker*, from February 1925 (and on nearly every anniversary issue since then)?

1. **Marilyn Monroe**. Her now-famous centerfold photo was actually repurposed from a nude calendar she posed for in 1949, just before breaking through as a certified star. Monroe was reportedly paid $50 for the original calendar shoot, and Hugh Hefner paid $500 to reprint the pictures—quite a bargain! (As for *Playboy*, Hefner was so unsure of the magazine's prospects that he didn't even bother printing the date on the first issue.)

2. **John Lennon**, appearing in a still from the movie *How I Won the War*. (Although *How I Won the War* wasn't terribly well received by critics, it's not without some degree of significance: while filming the movie, John Lennon first took to wearing his trademark round "granny" glasses.)

3. **Desiderio Alberto Arnaz IV** (better known as Desi Arnaz Jr.), accompanied by the headline "Lucy's $50,000,000 Baby." Yes, his parents were Lucille Ball and Desi Arnaz, arguably the biggest names in TV at the time. Ball's real-life pregnancy was mirrored in Lucy and Ricky Ricardo's fake life on *I Love Lucy*, with the entire TV-watching nation eagerly awaiting the birth of "Little Ricky." (Arnaz Jr. never actually portrayed Little Ricky on *I Love Lucy*, but he did go on to become an actor in his own right.)

4. The inaugural members of the Avengers were **Iron Man**, **The Incredible Hulk**, **Thor**, **Ant Man**, and **The Wasp**. (The first "cover villain" was Loki.) If you're wondering about a certain blond do-gooder named Captain America, he didn't join the team until issue #4.

5. **Charles Lindbergh**, who received the honor in recognition of his historic transatlantic solo flight in May of that year. In 1999, *Time* renamed the honor "Person of the Year" (though several women had been honored before then, each given the one-off title "Woman of the Year").

6. *Ms.* **magazine**. The world's most famous female superhero was drawn larger than life (à la the movie poster for *Attack of the 50 Foot Woman*) protecting a

city from warfare, beneath the headline "Wonder Woman for President" (it was an election year, after all). Cofounded by feminists Gloria Steinem and Dorothy Pitman Hughes, *Ms.* started life as an insert in *New York* magazine in 1971, when it featured the Hindu goddess Kali on its cover, before beginning its stand-alone run the following year.

7. She was the **cover model for the first *Sports Illustrated* "Swimsuit Issue,"** published in January 1964. Compared to the string bikinis (or less!) that models have worn in recent issues, Babette March's two-piece swimsuit looks downright modest.

8. **Eustace Tilley** is the nattily dressed gentlemen shown pondering a butterfly—or perhaps the butterfly is pondering him? The character was drawn by Rea Irvin (who also crafted *The New Yorker*'s signature logo), and though he didn't have a name at first—that came later in the year—Eustace Tilley quickly became the magazine's mascot.

Alfred E. Neuman didn't appear on the cover of *Mad* until issue 21 in 1955, back when it was still a comic book.

CHRIS

LIFETIME MOVIE OR NOT LIFETIME MOVIE?

BY DANA

I love Lifetime network movies; they're relatable to me as a woman, but also pretty cray-cray in a wonderfully over-the-top way. A good Lifetime Original Movie starring Meredith Baxter or Sela Ward is perfect for putting things in perspective when you have the flu. Yes, you feel terrible, but it could be *so* much worse.

Can you tell which Lifetime movies are real and which are just wishful thinking?

MOVIES

1. *A Deadly Adoption:* A couple takes in a pregnant woman in hopes of adopting her child.

2. *Abra-ca-baby!:* A magician copes with being pregnant while also headlining in Vegas.

3. *An Officer and a Murderer:* A military officer is suspected of murder.

4. *Aunt Flo's Got Her Groove Back:* An older woman finds love with a younger man in Aruba.

5. *Crowned and Dangerous:* A beauty queen is suspected of murder.

6. *Custody of the Heart:* A successful businesswoman fights for custody of her children.

7. *Dead Ringer: 1-800-Murder:* A plucky retiree investigates the suspicious murders of telemarketers.

8. *Flirting with Forty:* A 40-year-old woman finds love with a younger man in Hawaii.

9. *Good Girl Gone:* A woman fakes her death to escape her abusive husband.

Hint: twelve of these are real and eight are fake.

DANA

10. *The Grifter's Wife:* A woman unwittingly marries a con man and must decide whether to join in his scams.

11. *His and Her Christmas:* Two columnists from competing newspapers argue about Christmas.

12. *Hostile Makeover:* A supermodel is murdered in front of a fashion journalist.

13. *I Killed My BFF:* One young mother kills another.

14. *I Me Wed:* A woman marries herself.

15. *Lethal Seduction:* A mother must save her teenage son from a devious older woman.

16. *Me, Myself, & Di:* Stories from Princess Diana's personal assistant.

17. *Mrs. Nobody:* A woman finds herself after getting married.

18. *One Dave at a Time:* A woman is wooed by several men named Dave.

19. *Too Young to Be a Dad:* A woman must cope when her son becomes a teen father.

20. *Why I Wore Lipstick to My Mastectomy:* A woman must cope with breast cancer.

Real

1. *A Deadly Adoption*

3. *An Officer and a Murderer*

5. *Crowned and Dangerous*

6. *Custody of the Heart*

8. *Flirting with Forty*

11. *His and Her Christmas*

12. *Hostile Makeover*

13. *I Killed My BFF*

14. *I Me Wed*

15. *Lethal Seduction*

19. *Too Young to Be a Dad*

20. *Why I Wore Lipstick to My Mastectomy*

Fake

2. *Abra-ca-baby!*

4. *Aunt Flo's Got Her Groove Back*

7. *Dead Ringer: 1-800-Murder*

9. *Good Girl Gone*

10. *The Grifter's Wife*

16. *Me, Myself, & Di*

17. *Mrs. Nobody*

18. *One Dave at a Time*

SEQUEL-IZE ME

BY COLIN

When *The Godfather: Part II* won the 1974 Academy Award for Best Picture, it not only cemented Francis Ford Coppola's status as a preeminent director—it also legitimized the sequel. Once limited to low-budget serials and B-movies, sequels quickly became a staple of the major studios, commanding budgets that often exceeded those of the movies that spawned them.

Of course, it takes more than a familiar title to sell a sequel—you also need a great movie-poster tagline! Can you identify these 12 movie sequels, given only the taglines from their promotional posters?

TAGLINES

1. The toys are back in town.

2. Getting back was only the beginning.

3. First he fought for the crown; now he's fighting for the family jewels.

4. How far down does the rabbit hole go?

5. Why so serious?

6. Once…they made history. Now…they are history.

7. Someone has taken their love of sequels one step too far.

8. The second year begins.

9. At the end of the universe lies the beginning of vengeance.

10. The rematch of the century.

11. The perfect boyfriend. The perfect life. What could possibly go wrong?

12. There are some places in the universe you don't go alone.

1. *Toy Story 2*

2. *Back to the Future Part II*

3. *Austin Powers: The Spy Who Shagged Me*

4. *The Matrix Reloaded*

5. *The Dark Knight*

6. *Bill & Ted's Bogus Journey*

7. *Scream 2*

8. *Harry Potter and the Chamber of Secrets*

9. *Star Trek II: The Wrath of Khan*

10. *Rocky II*

11. *Bridget Jones: The Edge of Reason*

12. *Aliens*

THE PERFECT BAND NAME

BY DANA

～⚮～

Do you ever hear series of unlikely words and go, "That's totally going to be the name of my band?" Me, too. Look for my band "Bedtime Booger Bubble" (thanks, Karen!) dropping our debut album in 2030. In this quiz, I'll give you a few tidbits about a band's genre and name origins, and your job is to guess which band is being referenced. Rock on!

CLUES

1. Formed in 1972, this Swedish pop group's name is an acronym made from the initials of the band members' first names.

2. This American new wave rock band got its name from a particular style of beehive hairdo.

3. This British reggae/pop band named itself after a well-known U.K. governmental form.

4. This American rock band took its name from Radioactive Man's sidekick on *The Simpsons*.

5. This American rock band formed in 1995 and picked its name—meaning "the act or state of vanishing away"—from the dictionary.

6. Formed in 1967, this American rock band named itself after an early flatbed truck model.

7. This Irish new wave band got its name from Woody Guthrie's boyhood gang.

8. This Scottish indie pop band took its name from a TV show based on a 1965 children's book by French writer Cécile Aubry.

9. Founded in 1982, this Celtic punk band adapted a "cheeky" Irish phrase to use as its name.

10. The name of this English pop/rock band comes from a line in a book by American psychologist Arthur Janov.

11. Founded in 2009, this heavy metal band has the same name as a 1937 John Steinbeck novella.

12. This new wave band gets its name from the jerky movement that prisoners made when they were hanged at a particular prison.

1. **ABBA**. Their names are Agnetha Fältskog, Björn Ulvaeus, Benny Andersson, and Anni-Frid Lyngstad.

2. **The B-52s**. Two members of the band, Kate Pierson and Cindy Wilson, are known for sporting some pretty amazing beehives. The B-52 beehive hairdo gets its name from Boeing B-52 airplanes.

3. **UB40**. UB40 stands for Unemployment Benefit, Form 40. Though the British government doesn't use the form anymore, it's still well known and used in the U.K. to refer to unemployment claims in general.

4. **Fall Out Boy**. On *The Simpsons*, Radioactive Man's young sidekick is known as "Fallout Boy." In the episode "Radioactive Man," Milhouse Van Houten is cast as Fallout Boy in the Radioactive Man movie being shot in Springfield.

Game of Thrones actress Carice van Houten played a Van Houten cousin on a later episode of The Simpsons.

5. **Evanescence**. Previous names the band experimented with included "Childish Intentions" and "Stricken."

CHRIS

6. **REO Speedwagon**. The founder of the band heard about Ransom E. Olds (the founder of Oldsmobile) and his REO Speed Wagon in one of his college classes. Predecessor of the modern-day pickup truck, Speed Wagons were introduced in 1915 and were used as ambulances, fire trucks, and delivery trucks.

7. **The Boomtown Rats**. Bob Geldof got the name from Woody Guthrie's autobiography. As a child, Guthrie had been in a street gang in Oklahoma City, which became known as "Boomtown" after oil was discovered there in 1928.

8. **Belle & Sebastian**. Cécile Aubry's novel *Belle et Sébastien* is about a six-year-old boy named Sébastien and his Pyrenean Mountain Dog named Belle who live in the French Alps. The book spawned a French live-action TV show, a Japanese anime series, and two movies.

9. **The Pogues**. They were originally called Pogue Mahone, the anglicized version of Póg mo Thóin (in English: "Kiss My Ass"). They shortened that to The Pogues after people complained to the BBC.

10. **Tears for Fears**. The band's name was inspired by a line from *Prisoners of Pain,* a book on primal therapy written by Arthur Janov. The idea of primal therapy is that repressed pain can be resolved by re-experiencing and fully expressing it during therapy.

11. **Of Mice & Men**. John Steinbeck took the name for his book about migrant ranch workers from a line in the poem "To a Mouse," by Robert Burns: "The best-laid schemes o' mice an' men/ Gang aft agley." ("The best-laid plans of mice and men/ Go oft awry.")

12. **Spandau Ballet**. When the band was looking for a new name, a friend suggested "Spandau Ballet," which he'd seen written on the wall of a nightclub bathroom. Turns out this phrase has a pretty grisly backstory. Legend has it that the expression "Spandau Ballet" refers to the jerking bodies of Nazi War criminals hanged at Spandau Prison after World War II. Another similarly dark explanation is that it's slang for the twitching bodies caught on barbed wire and hit by Spandau machine guns during World War I.

BEEP ME MAYBE

BY CHRIS

I'm rollin' like a Playboy, beep beep | Just another page, just another freak.

So wrote noted popular songsmith Sir Mix-a-Lot in his 1989 hit "Beepers."

The brief life of the pager, or beeper—a device that could receive very limited, usually numerical wireless messages—remains a fascinating technological moment, presaging our current preoccupation with our smartphones. The behavior—obsessively checking one's portable messaging device, which doubled as a status symbol—was fully formed, even though the technology itself was laughably primitive. And since tech was advancing rapidly, beepers were obsolete in a brief period of time, leaving songs like Sir Mix-a-Lot's (and also "Skypager" by A Tribe Called Quest) as curious remnants of a specific era.

Pagers got their start in the 1950s, as a service for doctors in New York City. It began with a company named "Telanserphone," which they clearly came up with after many arduous minutes of work. They set up a radio antenna that could reach the entire Big Apple. It broadcast a single signal to the pagers, which were like one-way walkie-talkies. Doctors could listen in every hour to see if they heard their own personal code number, which was a signal that they should call their office. The code numbers were read off tiny pieces of filmstrip embedded in plastic sticks, and operators would put the sticks onto what basically looked like a bicycle chain inside a large machine. This would carry the sticks around in a loop, and the audio on each filmstrip would play as the stick passed the machine's reading device.[1]

Fast forward a few years, and pager technology has gotten cheaper and faster, eventually ending up in the hands of…teens. Schools wanted to ban pagers at first because they were associated with drug dealers. But eventually it became clear that kids were using them not only to communicate with each other, but also as fashion statements and status symbols.[2]

---

1. C. Ennis, "Pocket Radio Pages Doctors Night and Day," *Popular Science*, 158, no. 1 (January 1951): 104-105.
2. Jocelyn Stewart, "Chic Teen-Agers Keep in Touch with Beepers," *Los Angeles Times*, April 21, 1991, articles.la.times .com/1991-04-21/local/me-865_1_school-districts.

Want to make it seem like you're important? Wear a pager prominently so that it seems like someone may need to reach you at all times. It doesn't even matter if the beeper is an old, totally broken one you found in the trash—just make sure people can see it. One *New York Times* report said that kids would wear "small plastic boxes that look like beepers but are not."[3] Like the peacock's colorful plumage, the prominently displayed pager was part of a mating ritual for the early '90s male teen.

Pagers only displayed short strings of numbers, and why not? They were intended for businesspeople, to alert them to call a specific telephone number. But kids used pagers in school when they couldn't talk on the phone, so they had to develop numerical codes for various messages. The code "143," for example, meant "I love you"—derived from the number of letters in each word of the phrase. Turn "07734" upside-down, and it looks like "Hello."

There are still many lists of beeper codes on the Internet, although they may all disappear if Angelfire.com ever shuts down. Can you guess what these numerical codes translate to?

CODES

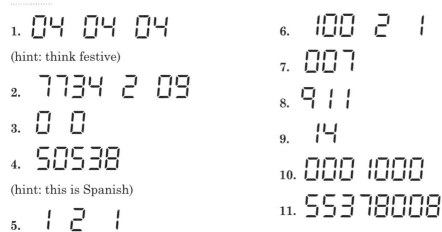

1. 04 04 04
(hint: think festive)

2. 7734 2 09

3. 0 0

4. 50538
(hint: this is Spanish)

5. 1 2 1

6. 100 2 1

7. 007

8. 911

9. 14

10. 000 1000

11. 5537 8008

---

3. Jonathan Rabinovitz, "Teen-Agers' Beepers: Communications as Fashion," *New York Times*, March 8, 1991, www.nytimes.com/1991/03/08/nyregion/teen-agers-beepers-communiciations-as-fashion.html.

1. 04 04 04 upside down is "Ho Ho Ho," meaning "Merry Christmas."

2. 7734 2 09 upside down-ish is "Go to hell." Gasp!

3. 0 0 is "Uh-oh!" You're in trouble now...

4. 50538 upside down is "Besos," or "Kisses" in Spanish.

5. 1 2 1 is "I need to talk to you," as in "We should speak one-to-one."

6. 100 2 1 is "Fat chance," as in "the odds are a hundred to one."

7. 007 is "It's a secret" or "I know a secret." (If you don't know why...)

8. Not trying to trick you: 911 means "emergency." (Although you and a teenage girl from the '90s may have a difference of opinion as to what constitutes an emergency.)

9. 14 upside-down is "Hi," for when you're too tired to punch in 07734.

10. 0001000 is a pictograph that means "I'm feeling alone." One *is* the loneliest number...

11. Flip 55378008 upside down and it spells (sigh) "Boobless." Here's a special answer-section bonus: this is the punch line to our favorite calculator joke. Get out a digital calculator and say to someone, as you punch in these numbers, "Dolly Parton's bra size was 69, and that was 2, 2, 2, big. So she took 51 diet pills, then went to see Dr. X, 8 times. Now she's..."—and you multiply 6922251 X 8, which is 55378008.

GETTING THAT LAST WORD IN

BY CHRIS

❧

The final lines of films are the last impression left with viewers (unless they stick around after the credits to see if there's one last scene with Samuel L. Jackson), and they're likely to carry that with them as they leave the theater. So, of course, they're chosen and written very carefully. Here are some of my favorite final lines from all-time classic films; I'll give you the final words, you name the movie.

FINAL LINES

1. "Throw that junk."

2. "I'm going to go home and sleep with my wife."

3. "I think this is the beginning of a beautiful friendship."

4. "Attaboy, Clarence."

5. "I was cured, all right."

6. "Hey everybody! We're all gonna get laid!"

7. "It's too bad she won't live. But then again, who does?"

8. "I love this town!"

9. "I don't have to see it, Dottie. I lived it."

10. "Where we're going, we don't need roads."

11. "As you wish."

12. "I get to live the rest of my life like a schnook."

1. *Citizen Kane* (followed by Kane's beloved sled Rosebud being thrown into an incinerator)

2. *Clue*

3. *Casablanca*

4. *It's a Wonderful Life*

5. *A Clockwork Orange*

6. *Caddyshack*

7. *Blade Runner*

8. *Ghostbusters*

9. *Pee Wee's Big Adventure*

10. *Back to the Future*

11. *The Princess Bride*

12. *Goodfellas*

REMEMBER THESE MOVIE QUOTES?

BY CHRIS

All of the following legendary movie quotes have something in common. Will you be able to figure it out? Do you feel lucky, punk?

QUOTES

1. "My momma always said: life is like a box of chocolates. You never know what you're gonna get."
   —*Forrest Gump*

2. "Hello, Clarice."
   —*The Silence of the Lambs*

3. "We're gonna need a bigger boat."
   —*Jaws*

4. "Mirror, mirror, on the wall—who is the fairest of them all?"
   —*Snow White and the Seven Dwarfs*

5. "Badges? We don't need no stinkin' badges!"
   —*The Treasure of the Sierra Madre*

6. "You want the truth? You can't handle the truth!"
   —*A Few Good Men*

7. "If you build it, they will come."
   —*Field of Dreams*

8. "Play it again, Sam."
   —*Casablanca*

9. "Luke, I am your father."
   —*The Empire Strikes Back*

10. "I'm king of the world!"
    —*Titanic*

11. "Are you trying to seduce me, Mrs. Robinson?"
    —*The Graduate*

These are some of the most famous movie quotes of all time. They're also wrong. Each is a popular misquote from the film in question. Don't feel bad if you didn't get it—these lines are quite often remembered and repeated differently than they were actually recited in their films. Here are the actual lines, with the oft-misquoted parts in italics:

1. "My momma always said: life *was* like a box of chocolates…"

2. "*Good evening,* Clarice."

3. "*You're* gonna need a bigger boat."

4. "*Magic* mirror on the wall—who is the fairest *one of* all?"

5. "Badges? *We ain't got no badges.* We don't need no *badges. I don't have to show you any* stinkin' badges!"

6. "You want *answers?*"
   "*I want the truth.*"
   "You can't handle the truth!"

7. "If you build it, *he* will come."

8. "Play it *once,* Sam, *for old times' sake.*"

9. "*No,* I am your father."

10. "I'm *the* king of the world!"

11. "Mrs. Robinson, *you're* trying to seduce me, *aren't you?*"

Oh, and there's even a misquote in the instructions. The correct line from *Dirty Harry* is, "You've got to ask yourself one question: 'Do I feel lucky?' Well, do ya, punk?"

WILLIAM SHAKE-YO'-BOOTY-SPEARE

BY KAREN

⤜⤛

William Shake-Yo'-Booty-Speare is back, and since the last quiz, he's learned how to rhyme. Is there anything the Bardy Mack can't do? He's rewritten more of his favorite party tunes into something approximating Elizabethan English. See if you can decipher the pop jams to which Big Willy Style is rockin' out.

LYRICS

1. *A jug of whiskey on mine fangs—it will clean and burn;*
   'tis time to part this evening, and I shall not return.

2. *I beckon thee, let sweetness cascade upon mine skin.*
   Call it your affection, that's what I desire within.

3. *Mine, mine, mine, mine melody hath strucketh with excess vigor;*
   Hence I hath chanteth, "O! Mine Maker."

4. *You there, good lad! Naught any reason for lament.*
   I say, good lad! Kneel up from that pavement.

5. *The Lady nabs mine riches, at times of down-and-out.*
   Aye! Her, a frivolous familiar of mine, without a doubt.
   O! A miner of gilded jewels, o'er the village wide.
   Her, a miner of mines, and of what is mine.

6. *Mine creamy concoction shall barken*
   wand'ring fellows to the garden.
   They clamor, 'Tis finer than thine.
   O Truth! 'Tis finer than thine.
   Instructions I shall deliver
   'pon payment of gold and silver.

1. *Before I leave brush my teeth with a bottle of Jack*
   'Cause when I leave for the night I ain't comin' back

   "Tik Tok" by Ke$ha

2. *Pour some sugar on me*
   In the name of love

   "Pour Some Sugar On Me" by Def Leppard

3. *My-my-my-my music hits me so hard*
   makes me say oh my Lord

   "U Can't Touch This" by MC Hammer

4. *Young man, there's no need to feel down*
   I said, young man, pick yourself off the ground

   "YMCA" by the Village People

5. *She take my money when I'm in need*
   Yeah she's a trifling friend indeed
   Oh she's a gold digger way over town
   that digs on me

   "Gold Digger" by Kanye West featuring Jamie Foxx

6. *My milkshake brings all the boys to the yard,*
   And they're like
   It's better than yours,
   Damn right it's better than yours,
   I can teach you,
   But I have to charge

   "Milkshake" by Kelis

A NUMBER OF PROBLEMS

BY KAREN

Recently, the whole *Good Job, Brain!* crew had to travel to Ohio for a wedding because Dana was a bridesmaid—again! She's **been in so many weddings as a bridesmaid**, it's ridiculous. When we arrived, we ended up witnessing a crazy accident in Ohio: **a train carrying an alien who'd landed on Earth got derailed!** Totally freaked out, we bailed and ended up in nearby Detroit, where Chris made us some extra money by **engaging in underground rap battles**. With funds in hand, we decided to splurge. We made our way to London, where we **had a run-in with a zombie infestation** and had to hide out in the Underground.

Making a heroic escape, we boarded a plane for Japan. But our troubles weren't over, because a local village asked us to **help find a group of heroes to defend them against marauding bandits**. Sheesh! Once the village was safe, we got back home to America, but since we'd depleted all our funds, Colin had to use his giant brain to **count cards and win big at blackjack** in Las Vegas.

All in all, it was a crazy weekend! How would you **sum up** our adventure?

ANSWERS

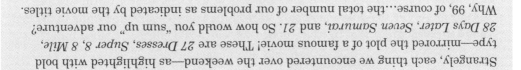

Strangely, each thing we encountered over the weekend—as highlighted with bold type—mirrored the plot of a famous movie! These are *27 Dresses*, *Super 8*, *8 Mile*, *28 Days Later*, *Seven Samurai*, and *21*. So how would you "sum up" our adventure? Why, 99, of course…the total number of our problems as indicated by the movie titles.

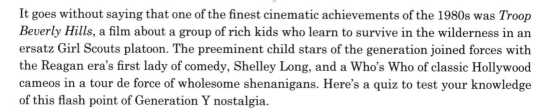

WILDERNESS GIRLS

BY CHRIS

It goes without saying that one of the finest cinematic achievements of the 1980s was *Troop Beverly Hills*, a film about a group of rich kids who learn to survive in the wilderness in an ersatz Girl Scouts platoon. The preeminent child stars of the generation joined forces with the Reagan era's first lady of comedy, Shelley Long, and a Who's Who of classic Hollywood cameos in a tour de force of wholesome shenanigans. Here's a quiz to test your knowledge of this flash point of Generation Y nostalgia.

QUESTIONS

1. According to the Girl Scouts of America—an organization that had nothing to do with this film—the most popular Girl Scout cookie is the Thin Mint. What is the second most popular?

2. The actress who played Shelley Long's fictional daughter went on to have a successful music career, both as a solo artist and as a member of an indie band. Who is she?

3. Long's fictional ex-husband in *Troop Beverly Hills* was played by a veteran actor best known for playing the role of Hayden Fox on what sitcom?

4. One of the Wilderness Girls was played by Emily Schulman, best known for her role in a TV series with the main character "Voice Input Child Identicant." What was the name of that TV show?

5. Another Wilderness Girl was played by an actress who went on to get stabbed to death in an episode of *ER*. Who was she?

6. After later roles in *Spy Kids* and *Sin City*, Wilderness Girl actress Carla Gugino became one of the top-grossing female stars of the last 20 years, according to the last time I checked *Wikipedia*. In what comic-book movie did she play Sally Jupiter?

GOOD JOB, **BRAIN!**

7. Mary Gross played Long's troop co-leader. She was on *Saturday Night Live* for five years, but I remember her best from a comedy film about the FBI in which she starred alongside Rebecca DeMornay. What is the film title?

8. Which Wilderness Girl actress went on to write an autobiography called *Stori Telling*?

9. What celebrity made a cameo in *Troop Beverly Hills*, jogging through a scene singing her 1959 hit "Tall Paul"?

10. A guy who used to go by the name Ferdinand Lewis Alcindor, Jr., made a brief appearance in this film. Under what name was he credited?

11. True *Troop Beverly Hills* fans will surely remember Velda, the evil leader of the rival Wilderness Girls troop. This was actually the final film appearance for that actress, Betty Thomas. She went on to be one of the highest-grossing female film directors ever. What 1995 smash comedy hit about an odd family reunited Thomas as director with Long as actress?

1. This is sort of a trick question, since Girl Scout cookies are often known by different names in different parts of the country! Depending on where you live, the second most popular cookie might be called either **Samoas** or **Caramel deLites**.

2. It's **Jenny Lewis**, the quintessential Toys "R" Us kid (and Rilo Kiley frontwoman).

3. *Coach*; the actor was Craig T. Nelson.

4. *Small Wonder*. Emily didn't play V.I.C.I. the robot, though; that was Tiffany Brissette. Emily played annoying next-door neighbor, Harriet.

5. **Kellie Martin**, who also starred in *Life Goes On* on TV.

6. *Watchmen*. The book is better.

7. *Feds*. Mary Gross is my comedy hero.

8. **Tori Spelling**, of course. (She was in the rival Wilderness Girls troop.)

9. **Annette Funicello**, followed closely by a jogging Frankie Avalon.

10. **Kareem Abdul-Jabbar**.

11. *The Brady Bunch Movie*. More recently, Thomas directed *Alvin and the Chipmunks: The Squeakquel*.

FUN TIME VOCAB CORNER

BY DANA

SNARGE

noun | /snärj/

n. The goo that results when a bird and a plane, especially a plane's turbine engine, collide; a bird smoothie.

Etymology: A portmanteau of the words "snot" and "garbage,"[4] snarge was likely coined by the researchers who prepare bird specimens at the Smithsonian Institution in Washington, DC.

Example: "The snarge on the plane's engine gave investigators an important clue about why it crashed."

---

4. Michael M. Phillips, "In Battle on Birds, Air Force Deploys a Secret Weapon," *Wall Street Journal*, January 4, 2008, www.wsj.com/articles/SB1199402/30/9/66/31.

TV REBUS TIME!

BY CHRIS

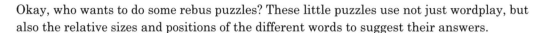

Okay, who wants to do some rebus puzzles? These little puzzles use not just wordplay, but also the relative sizes and positions of the different words to suggest their answers.

For example:

HOUSE
<u>　　　　　　　</u>
THE PRAIRIE

Answer: *Little House on the Prairie*

LOVE

Answer: *Big Love*

Like both of these examples, the answers to all the following puzzles are the names of television series. Can you solve them all? Warning: some of them might get TEALITTLENSE (a little intense)!

1.

ALL CREATURES

ALL CREATURES

2.

THE PRICE

3.

PEOPLE

WORLD

4.

THEFAMIALLLY

5.

COMFORT
CLOSE COMFORT
CLOSE COMFORT
COMFORT

6.

THE _____

S

7.

2

COOKCOOKCOOKCOOKCOOKCOOKCOOK
COOKCOOKCOOKCOOKCOOKCOOKCOOK
COOKCOOKCOOKCOOKCOOKCOOKCOOK
COOKCOOKCOOKCOOKCOOKCOOKCOOK
COOKCOOKCOOKCOOKCOOKCOOKCOOK
COOKCOOKCOOKCOOKCOOKCOOKCOOK

8.

HEAVEN
HEAVEN
HEAVEN
HEAVEN
HEAVEN
HEAVEN
→ HEAVEN ←
HEAVEN
HEAVEN

9.

MAN ON EARTH
MAN ON EARTH
MAN ON EARTH
MAN ON EARTH
MAN ON EARTH
→ MAN ON EARTH ←

10.

MINUTEMINUTEMINUTEMINUTEMINUTEMINUTE
MINUTEMINUTEMINUTEMINUTEMINUTEMINUTE
MINUTEMINUTEMINUTEMINUTEMINUTEMINUTE
MINUTEMINUTEMINUTEMINUTEMINUTEMINUTE
MINUTEMINUTEMINUTEMINUTEMINUTEMINUTE
MINUTEMINUTEMINUTEMINUTEMINUTEMINUTE
MINUTEMINUTEMINUTEMINUTEMINUTEMINUTE
MINUTEMINUTEMINUTEMINUTEMINUTEMINUTE
MINUTEMINUTEMINUTEMINUTEMINUTEMINUTE
MINUTEMINUTEMINUTEMINUTEMINUTEMINUTE

11.

FIRE
―――――
GRACE

12.

WONDER

13.

GERALDO **AT**

14.

ᴘ ᴀ I N S

15.

―――――――――
FOOT FOOT FOOT
FOOT FOOT FOOT

16.

L
A
S
T
M
A
N

SPALOSTCE

17.

R THE **R**

18.

BOUND
A
N
D

19.

BO4DY

20.

N
W
O
R
G
L
L
A

21.

EKIRTS

22.

1. *All Creatures Great and Small*

2. *The Price Is Right*

3. *Little People, Big World*

4. *All in the Family*

5. *Too Close for Comfort*

6. *The Leftovers*

7. *Too Many Cooks*

8. *7th Heaven*

9. *Last Man on Earth*

10. *60 Minutes*

11. *Grace Under Fire*

12. *Small Wonder*

13. *Geraldo at Large*

14. *Growing Pains*

15. *Six Feet Under*

16. *Last Man Standing*

17. *Lost in Space*

18. *The Inbetweeners*

19. *Eastbound and Down*

20. *Foreign Body*

21. *All Grown Up*

22. *Strike Back*

1992 AT THE MOVIES!

BY CHRIS

The 65th Annual Academy Awards honored films released during the year 1992. And let me tell you, there were lots of excellent (or at least very weird) movies released that year. There were in fact so many that I wrote a whole quiz about 1992's motion picture bonanza. Can you remember 1992? Were you even alive in 1992? If you weren't, I'd like to ask that you please not remind me how old I am.

QUESTIONS

1. Perhaps the most enduring film released in 1992 was Disney's *Aladdin*. It won two Oscars: Best Original Score and Best Original Song, for "A Whole New World." What other *Aladdin* tune was also nominated for Best Original Song?

2. Another 1992 film had two songs nominated in the Best Original Song category, and its soundtrack album became the best-selling soundtrack album of all time. What film was it?

3. In 1992, Al Pacino became the sixth person to receive nominations as Best Actor and Best Supporting Actor in the same year, for playing Lieutenant Colonel Frank Slade and Ricky Roma, respectively. Name the two films.

4. Susan Sarandon was nominated as Best Actress for her role in what film, based on a true story about a combination of oleic and erucic acids?

5. What legal drama directed by Rob Reiner was nominated as Best Picture?

6. Robert Downey, Jr., was nominated as Best Actor for playing what other actor?

7. Clint Eastwood took home Best Picture and Best Director awards for what film?

8. *Howards End*, *Scent of a Woman*, *Enchanted April*, *The Player*, and *A River Runs through It* were the nominees for what award?

9. Boy George sang the title tune for the winner of Best Original Screenplay. What film was this?

10. Awards for Best Makeup and Best Costume Design went to what Francis Ford Coppola–helmed romantic horror film?

11. Besides his turn as the Genie in *Aladdin*, Robin Williams was the star of what live-action 1992 film that also featured Michael Gambon, Joan Cusack, and LL Cool J?

12. Finally, the winner of the Best Visual Effects award—beating out *Alien 3* and *Batman Returns*—was what dark fantasy comedy starring Meryl Streep and Goldie Hawn?

ANSWERS

1. "Friend Like Me," performed by the great Robin Williams.

2. *The Bodyguard*, which remains one of a very few albums to sell more than 40 million copies. The two songs were "Run to You" and "I Have Nothing." (The most famous song from the film, "I Will Always Love You," wasn't nominated because it wasn't original—it was a Whitney Houston cover of a Dolly Parton song.)

3. *Scent of a Woman* and *Glengarry Glen Ross*. (He won for *Scent of a Woman*.)

4. *Lorenzo's Oil*. (The oil in question is a treatment for adrenoleukodystrophy, or ALD.)

5. *A Few Good Men*.

6. Charlie Chaplin, in *Chaplin*.

7. *Unforgiven*.

8. Best Adapted Screenplay.

9. *The Crying Game*.

10. *Bram Stoker's Dracula*.

11. *Toys*.

12. *Death Becomes Her*.

WEIRD SCIENCE, WEIRDER ANIMALS

HERE ARE THE ANIMALS, INVENTIONS, **AND** CRAZY SCIENCE THAT WE LOVE MOST.

YOU'LL FIND WE'RE PARTICULARLY FASCINATED WITH STUFF THAT COMES OUT OF ANIMALS' BUTTS. IT'S NOT JUST POOP! (A LOT OF IT IS POOP.)

CELEBRITAXONOMY

BY KAREN

Biologists! They're just like us! Nature experts sure love their pop culture. Here are a few species of animals named after celebrities—and for good reason!

Agra schwarzeneggeri

(Discovered in 2002 in Costa Rica.) This particular species of carabid beetle sports a pair of beefy middle femora that look like the bulging biceps of bodybuilder-turned-actor-turned-politician Arnold Schwarzenegger.

Scaptia beyonceae

(Named in 2011.) Native to Australia, this horsefly is anything but plain. Named after the irreplaceable Beyoncé Knowles, the fly has a bootylicious golden behind. The only samples collected so far have been female.

There's also a spider named for Schwarzenegger called *Predatoroonops schwarzeneggeri*. Yes, it was named that because it looks like the monster from *Predator*.

DANA

Cirolana mercuryi

(Discovered in 2004.) This accordion-like crustacean was found off Bawe Island of Zanzibar (now part of Tanzania), where Queen's legendary frontman Freddie Mercury was born. Mercury also has a whole other genus of animals named after him: Mercurana frogs were discovered in 2012 in the mountains near the hill station of Panchgani in India, where Mercury spent his childhood.

Aleiodes shakirae

(Discovered in 2014 in Ecuador.) Wherever, whenever this small parasitic wasp injects her egg into a caterpillar, the baby wasp larva will slowly eat its host from the inside, causing the caterpillar to do a hypnotic twisty dance like Colombian superstar Shakira.

Barbaturex morrisoni

(Fossils discovered in Myanmar in 1970s, analyzed and named in 2013.) "I am the Lizard King, I can do anything." Jim Morrison, frontman of The Doors, wrote this line in a poem that appeared on one of the band's album sleeves. (That's back when music came on vinyl discs, kids.) Fitting, since the Barbaturex is an extinct GIANT LIZARD that probably measured up to six feet long.

Dendropsophus ozzyi

(Discovered in 2014.) This tiny frog, less than an inch long, can wail...but that's not why it's named after Ozzy Osbourne. The male frogs are known to make an abnormally loud scream that sounds a lot like a bat screech. And, well, Ozzy famously once had a heady run-in with a bat that was thrown on stage by a fan at a concert. Ozzy bit the bat's entire head off, though he later said he thought it was a fake rubber bat. RIP Concert Bat—never 4get.

A VERY AVERAGE HUMAN BODY BY THE NUMBERS

BY DANA

We all have human bodies, I hope (for this quiz, I'm assuming that you're a human and not an unusually clever dog), but we might not all have *average* human bodies. I, for example, never grew wisdom teeth, so I have four fewer teeth than the average adult human. There's definitely some wiggle room in the exact number of things a human body might have, but there is an average number for most things. How familiar are you with the specifics of an average human body?

QUESTIONS

1. How many pairs of ribs do most humans have?

    a. 6

    b. 12

    c. 18

2. How many teeth do most adults have?

    a. 28

    b. 32

    c. 34

3. How many pints of blood are in the average adult body?

    a. 6

    b. 10

    c. 20

4. How many bones are there in the average adult skeleton?

    a. 185

    b. 206

    c. 272

5. How many pinnae does the average human have?

    a. 1

    b. 2

    c. 10

6. How many lunulae does the average human have?

    a. 2

    b. 20

    c. 2,000

7. How many taste buds does the average human tongue have?

    a. 5 to 8

    b. 2,000 to 8,000

    c. 120,000 to 170,000

8. How much does an average adult brain weigh?

    a. 1 pound

    b. 3 pounds

    c. 5 pounds

If you always picked the middle answer, you did very well!

1. **(b)** Most humans have 12 pairs of ribs, or 24 individual ribs. Contrary to popular belief, men and women have the same number of ribs.

2. **(b)** Most adult humans have 32 teeth: eight incisors, four canines, eight premolars, eight molars, and four wisdom teeth.

3. **(b)** According to the American Red Cross, the average adult has 10 pints of blood. During blood donation, about one pint is drawn.

4. **(b)** There are 206 bones in the average adult body, while an average baby has about 300 bones! Many of these additional bones are in the skull and spine, and they fuse together as the baby grows older.

5. **(b)** The pinna is the part of the ear that's outside of your head (versus the parts inside your head, such as the canal and eardrum). Average humans have two of them.

6. **(b)** The lunulae are the crescent-shaped whitish areas at the beds of fingernails and toenails. The average number of fingernails and toenails is 20, so that's also the average number of lunulae.

7. **(b)** The average human tongue has between 2,000 and 8,000 taste buds.[5] There's a huge variability in how many taste buds people have. Children, for example, tend to have more. People who smoke tend to have fewer. This is, however, a quiz about averages.

8. **(b)** The average adult human brain weighs about three pounds. For all the unusually clever dogs taking this quiz, an average dog's brain weighs about 72 grams, or 0.16 pound.[6]

---

5. Reginald Chapman, "Taste bud," *Encyclopedia Britannica*, last updated April 22, 2016, accessed April 28, 2016, www.britannica.com/science/taste-bud.
6. Eric H. Chudler, "Brain Facts and Figures," University of Washington, last modified April 10, 2016, accessed April 28, 2016, https://faculty.washington.edu/chudler/facts.html.

THE BIG FIVE

BY DANA

Maybe you've noticed that we at *Good Job, Brain!* love animals and animal-related trivia. For some reason, a kind of dark, animal-related trivia topic comes up frequently in trivia competitions: "The Big Five" or "The Big Five Game." Basically, The Big Five is a list of the five most difficult animals to hunt on foot in Africa. The term comes from big-game hunters, who wanted a super-braggy way to talk about their trophies (I assume). We always had trouble remembering which animals are included in the Big Five. We knew that it was a list of dangerous animals in Africa, but Africa's a big place with lots of badass animals. Which ones made the cut? There had to be a mnemonic for remembering them. There wasn't, but we came up with one!

"Leaping Liberace's Elegant Rhinestone Cape!"

That is:

- **Le**opard (African leopard)

- **Li**on (African lion)

- **Ele**phant (African elephant)

- **Rhin**oceros (black and white rhinos)

- **Cape** buffalo

Much like a formidable Big Five animal, Liberace was at his most ferocious leaping across the stage in one of his many (MANY) elegant rhinestone capes.

Fun Fact: Liberace was such a great customer of the Austrian cut glass company Swarovski that they gifted him with the largest rhinestone in the world—115,000 carats, or 50.6 pounds!

THE FLYING TAILOR

BY COLIN

We love talking about inventors on *Good Job, Brain!* For me, the appeal is that great inventors don't fear failure—they embrace it. So allow me to share a story about Franz Reichelt, a man who embraced failure so hard he didn't know when to let go.

Reichelt was a tailor by trade who moved to in Paris in the late 1890s. Around the turn of the century, he became fascinated with airplanes. This wasn't unusual in itself; it was the dawn of the aviation age, and airplanes captured the public's imagination. But Reichelt was obsessed with aviation safety—in particular, parachutes.

Early airplanes were relatively fragile, and accidents often ended with dead pilots. Rudimentary parachutes existed, but they were cumbersome and unreliable at low altitudes. By 1910 Reichelt had dedicated himself to creating a practical parachute for the average pilot.

Reichelt was naturally handy with fabrics and pattern construction. Everything else he learned via trial and error...and error. He had some promising early experiments with wing-based designs, which he tested by attaching to dummies and dropping them from the upper floors of his apartment building. (Of course, a dummy won't complain about a rough landing, but you work with the volunteers you have.)

In 1911, the prestigious Aero-Club announced a prize of 10,000 francs for the inventor of a portable emergency parachute. Reichelt saw his golden opportunity, even though he'd have to drastically reduce the weight of his prototype to meet the contest's weight limit. Around this time, Reichelt stopped testing with dummies and began testing with a live person: himself.

It would be charitable to say things went poorly. He suffered hard landings from as high as 30 feet, and once he even broke his leg. Undaunted, he soldiered on. Eventually, Reichelt was so certain he'd claim the prize that he secured permission to stage a public demonstration using the lower deck of the Eiffel Tower.

On February 4, 1912, Reichelt arrived at the tower bright and early, ready to show off his custom parachute suit. Everyone expected him to use a dummy, but at the last minute he donned the parachute himself. With his friends watching nervously, Reichelt approached the railing. He had no nets, no ropes, no backup—nothing but confidence and a funny-looking suit. He checked the wind and paused to compose himself. Then he stepped off the edge, spread his arms...and plummeted 185 feet to his death.

His parachute never fully deployed, limply fluttering as he fell. In the aftermath, the police made it clear they'd only authorized Reichelt to drop a dummy, absolving themselves of any negligence in his death. The newspapers had a sensational story, but didn't show much sympathy for our poor aspiring flyer.

So why is Franz Reichelt remembered today? In no small part, it's because the event I just described was captured on film! Reichelt wanted ample coverage of his test, and boy, did he get it: two cameras documented the jump, from above and below. In recent years, clips of his "flight" have found new life on the Internet, in the form of YouTube videos and animated GIFs. But let's not remember Reichelt for his last mistake. Let's remember him as a man who was terminally unafraid of failure.

ANIMAL SECRETION SPOTLIGHT: BOMBARDIER BEETLE

BY KAREN

Our human butts are so boring. We sit on them, and then we use them to poop. That's about it. But the bombardier beetle—*hoo boy*—its butt is a full-blown weapon. The average bombardier beetle is less than an inch long, but its tiny body is packed with a chemical punch. When aggravated, the beetle will eject a spray of hot, hot, *hot* liquid from the butt end (abdomen) of its body. Not leak. Not secrete. *Eject*, with magnificent power and pressure. The beetle even has the ability to aim the spray by controlling the tip of its abdomen. All of this is made possible by an exothermic reaction of chemicals inside the beetle's body.

HOW DOES IT HAPPEN?

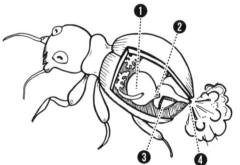

1. Two chemical liquids are produced and sit in a storage chamber.

2. When it's game time, the muscles cause valves to open and release the liquids into a reaction chamber.

3. The reaction chamber is lined with *catalases*—enzymes that act as catalysts for the reaction.

4. Once the liquids and catalases meet, the liquid heats almost to boiling, turning a portion into gas. With an explosive pop sound, hot liquid sprays from the beetle's butt.

You may wonder: "Well, wouldn't the beetle die from all this extreme heat inside its body?" Nope! The lining of the reaction chamber can withstand the mini-explosion, and the pressure of the ejection helps close the valves to the storage chamber so that the near-boiling liquid doesn't backfire. This protects the rest of the beetle's internal organs. And all of this happens in a fraction of a second, in a space only one millimeter wide. So, yeah. We humans have boring, unimpressive butts.

SCARCE HAIRS

BY DANA

❧

So who here really loves removing their body hair? ...Nobody? Well, society says we have to "maintain proper grooming standards," so I guess we just have to deal. Here's a quiz about our Sisyphean attempts to deny our mammalian heritage. Woo!

QUESTIONS

1. What brand of razor says it's "a choice for every goddess"?

2. Which hair removal product consisting of honey, molasses, sugar, and lemon juice was named for its inventor's daughter?

3. What is the name of the electrical device used to remove hair by mechanically grasping multiple hairs simultaneously and pulling them out?

4. The Arabic word for this type of hair removal is *khite*, and it has been widely practiced in the Eastern world for more than 6,000 years. What is it commonly known as in the U.S.?

5. What hair removal company used The Royal Teens' song "Short Shorts" to advertise its product in the 1970s?

6. What's the name for the process in which hair is destroyed with electrical probes?

7. What's the name for skin irritation that appears a few minutes after shaving?

8. Which pop singer's name does Steve Carell's character yell out when getting his chest waxed in the film *The 40-Year-Old Virgin*?

9. True or False: shaving causes hair to grow back thicker and coarser.

10. Does the word "depilation" refer to hair above the surface of the skin or below the surface of the skin?

1. **Venus Razors**. Venus is the Roman goddess of love.

2. **Nad's**. Sue Ismiel developed Nad's in 1992 when her daughter Natalie (aka "Nads") wanted to remove the hair from her arms.

3. **Epilator**. I can tell you from personal experience that this is very painful.

4. **Threading**. Thin thread is folded in two, twisted, and rolled over hair to catch it up and pull it out.

5. **Nair**. The song "Short Shorts" hit #3 on the U.S. *Billboard* charts in 1958, then got another surge of popularity when the Nair commercials aired in the 1970s.

6. **Electrolysis**. This is the only permanent hair removal method recognized by the Food and Drug Administration.

7. **Razor burn**. To help prevent razor burn, keep the skin moist, use a sharp blade, and practice proper shaving technique.

8. **Kelly Clarkson**. In the movie, Steve Carell's real chest hair was waxed off. He said it was one of the most painful things he's ever experienced.

9. **False**. Cutting the hair doesn't make it thicker, but it might seem that way because hair that has never been cut tends to taper at the ends.

10. **"Depilation"** refers to hair removal above the surface of the skin. "Epilation" refers to removal below the surface of the skin.

ONE HUMP OR TWO?

BY DANA

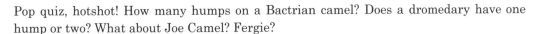

Pop quiz, hotshot! How many humps on a Bactrian camel? Does a dromedary have one hump or two? What about Joe Camel? Fergie?

Here's how we keep our camels straight.

- **Bactrian:** starts with *B*, and like a capital *B*, it has two humps.
- **Dromedary:** starts with the letter *D*, and like that letter, it has one hump.

The camel on the front of a box of Camel cigarettes is a dromedary, so it has one hump. Oddly enough, former mascot Joe Camel has no humps.

Though Fergie sings about her humps in the Black Eyed Peas song "My Humps," she never specifies an exact number. We can safely guess at least two.

TIME FLIES LIKE AN ARROW; URINAL FLIES LIKE PEE

BY CHRIS

If you were to go into a men's bathroom at John F. Kennedy Airport's Terminal 4 and look at all the urinals, you'd probably want to get a new hobby. But you'd also notice something interesting: on the surface of each urinal bowl, the image of a tiny housefly.

If you were to reach out and touch that fly—which I am not for a second suggesting that you do—you'd find that it was not a sticker or decal, but actually engraved into the porcelain!

What's the deal? Apparently, urinal flies reduce "spillage" by something like 80 percent. That's a whole lot less pee splashing out onto the floor. Why does it work? Apparently, just giving people a target to aim at is enough to turn anything, including public urination, into a fun game. Guys see a fly, they have to hit the fly.

If you're a bar owner or manage a public bathroom, you can actually buy specialized "waterproof" fly decals to stick onto urinals. I just wish my university had used these in the co-ed dorm bathrooms.

KAREN

National Public Radio reported that the JFK flies were modeled after similar ones in Amsterdam's Schiphol Airport.[7] Unfortunately, you may not be able to see the ones at JFK anymore, as the bathrooms have recently been earmarked for remodeling, sans flies. Too bad for the poor janitors—and you, if you've ever had to gymnastically straddle a puddle of a hundred other dudes' pee.

I carry a bag of flies with me at all times for this purpose.

COLIN

---

7. Robert Krulwich, "There's a Fly in My Urinal," National Public Radio, December 19, 2009, www.npr.org/templates/story/story.php?storyId=121310977.

GOOD JOB, BRAIN!

CHRISTMAS WITH BUGS

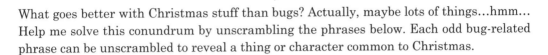

BY DANA

What goes better with Christmas stuff than bugs? Actually, maybe lots of things…hmm… Help me solve this conundrum by unscrambling the phrases below. Each odd bug-related phrase can be unscrambled to reveal a thing or character common to Christmas.

BUGS

1. CASUAL ANTS

2. TERMITES CRASH

3. SHYEST NONFAT WORM

4. THIN LEG NITS

5. NEAT IVY INSECT

6. PUSHIER OLDER REDDENED HORNET

7. ROGUISH GARDEN BEE

8. CALM ROACH STIRS

9. A CUTER TICK NURSE

10. A FRUMPY AIR SLUG

1. SANTA CLAUS

2. CHRISTMAS TREE

3. FROSTY THE SNOWMAN

4. SILENT NIGHT

5. NATIVITY SCENE

6. RUDOLPH THE RED-NOSED REINDEER

7. GINGERBREAD HOUSE

8. CHRISTMAS CAROL

9. NUTCRACKER SUITE

10. SUGAR PLUM FAIRY

SPY CAT!

BY COLIN

Let's travel back in time to the 1960s. It was the height of the Cold War, and relations between the U.S. and the Soviet Union could be described, at best, as "tensely suspicious." In an effort to stay one step ahead of the Soviets, agents at the Central Intelligence Agency were busy developing all sorts of spy technology, from the straightforward to the sublimely absurd. (If nothing else, the Cold War proved that when you have virtually unlimited funds and an army of imaginative, paranoid people, you can accomplish truly astounding things.)

I should mention now that this story does not have a particularly happy ending. It does, however, involve two of the things I love most in the world: spy gadgets and cats.

In a move that even Ian Fleming, the creator of superspy James Bond, might have deemed too far-fetched to believe, the CIA established a covert research program named "Project Acoustic Kitty."[8] And believe it or not, the goal was to turn cats into spies. Not the fedora-and-trench-coat variety, mind you—though that would be really freaking cute—but the mobile eavesdropping variety. What the CIA had in mind was implanting microphones and radio transmitters into cats and training them to target suspected spies in public settings. (Because what animal is easier to work with than the cat, am I right?)

So the CIA "recruited" at least one cat (I imagine it was a very short pitch), and the plan was underway. Agents had a veterinary surgeon implant a custom-made radio transmitter at the base of the cat's skull and a microphone in the cat's ear canal. A fine wire antenna ran out from the transmitter and along the cat's body, woven

8. Charlotte Edwardes, "CIA Recruited Cat to Bug Russians," *The Telegraph*, published November 4, 2001, accessed April 2016, www.telegraph.co.uk/news/northamerica/usa/1361462/CIA-recruited-cat-to-bug-Russians.html.

into her fur all the way to her tail. Despite the *Frankenstein* overtones, it really was an impressive feat: it was critical to design a system that wouldn't irritate the cat or be physically disrupted during the cat's routine cleaning.[9] Miniature batteries and components were required because, you know, the whole system had to fit inside a cat.

As crazy as it sounds, early lab tests actually went pretty well. Agents were able to train the cat to target locations a short distance away and stay put for brief periods. And on the technology side, they were able to overcome a variety of feline challenges, not the least of which was the cat's tendency to get distracted while hungry. Somehow, some way, Project Acoustic Kitty advanced to a final field test in the real world.

On the day of the test, agents packed up their fancy cat-detecting surveillance van and headed to a park near the Soviet embassy in Washington, DC, with the goal of eavesdropping on two men sitting on a park bench. The van parked. The door opened. The cat stepped out into the street. And the cat was promptly run over by a taxi.

I'm happy to report that this was the first and last field test of Project Acoustic Kitty. With a total project cost as high as $20 million, there wasn't much to show for it aside from a deceased feline agent (and presumably a whole mess of cat scratches). Although they were proud of the achievements they'd made in training cats, CIA officials decided their money was better spent on more traditional forms of spycraft, and by 1967 the project had been canceled. (At least one former CIA official says the cat was never hit by a car and actually lived a happy life after having the surveillance gear removed. But if you believe that, I have a cat-detecting van I'd like to sell you.)

Rest in peace, Acoustic Kitty. Your sacrifice to our nation's security is not forgotten.

---

9. Emily Anthes, "How the CIA Tried to Turn a Cat into a Cyborg Spy," *Popular Science*, published May 8, 2013, accessed April 2016, www.popsci.com/science/article/2013-05/cias-cyborg-cat.

EXTREME ANIMALS

BY COLIN

Record books aren't just for people—animals have some mighty fine achievements of their own to brag about. In this quiz we'll explore the extremes of the animal world, from the super-speedy to the super-scary.

QUESTIONS

1. What is the fastest land animal?

2. What is the largest animal on Earth?

3. What is the fastest animal in the air?

4. What is the world's most venomous animal (meaning it bites or stings)?

5. What is the fastest-swimming animal?

6. What animal is the world's fastest digger?

7. What is the world's most poisonous animal (to eat or touch)?

8. What is the oldest single animal on record? (Hint: it has a shell—in fact, it has two.)

1. **Cheetah**. Not a trick question—with a peak speed of more than 60 miles per hour, the cheetah is still the fastest land animal, as you probably learned in elementary school. In 2012, a cheetah named Sarah at the Cincinnati Zoo was clocked covering 100 meters in a blistering 5.95 seconds. In comparison, the fastest time recorded by human world record holder Usain Bolt over the same distance is 9.58 seconds. (No word on whether Sarah was docked for a tailwind.)

2. **Blue whale**. The largest animal ever to have existed, measuring up to 100 feet long and weighing as much as 200 tons. To put that in perspective, an African elephant (the largest living land animal) weighs "only" about seven tons on the high side. It's because we can't easily see them up close that we forget how spectacularly massive blue whales are!

3. **Peregrine falcon**. The peregrine is an airborne hunter, noted for its high-speed diving attack, or "stoop."[10] During a stoop, the peregrine smashes into its target from above, stunning and disabling the prey. Speeds in excess of 200 miles per hour have been recorded during peregrine dives, technically making this the fastest animal on Earth. That said, I feel that gravity should take some of the credit here, you know? (For what it's worth, the fastest bird in sustained, level flight is generally agreed to be the white-throated needletail, also called the spine-tailed swift.)

4. **Box jellyfish**. The dubious distinction of being Earth's most venomous animal goes to the box jellyfish—specifically, the "sea wasp" species, native to the coastal waters of Australia and nearby regions.

The Germans were known to employ a team of extraordinarily trained homing pigeons during World War II. These pigeons would carry classified information from base to base with little chance of detection. Not to be outdone, the British Royal Air Force also trained some birds. It just so happens that *their* birds were freaking peregrine falcons, so they could hunt and take down enemy messenger pigeons. The falcon squad had a cool name, too: Interceptor Unit No. 2. (Unit No. 1 was a fleet of actual interceptor aircrafts.)

KAREN

---

10. Max Hunn, "Teaching School for Falcons," *Popular Mechanics* 107, no. 5 (May 1957): 83.

Their venom is so powerful and the agony it causes so intense that sting victims can go into cardiac arrest even before making it to shore. Although most stings aren't fatal, a high-enough dose of the venom can cause death in as little as two minutes if untreated. (First aid for a box jellyfish sting calls for treating the area with vinegar to counteract any undischarged nematocysts—tiny, dart-like, venom injectors.)

5. **Sailfish**. This flashy, streamlined fish just *looks* fast, doesn't it? Prized game for sport fishers, sailfish can crank it up to 68 miles per hour out in the open water. The eye-catching "sails" running along their spines are normally folded down while swimming, then extended when the fish feel threatened or excited.

6. **Badger**. Thanks to their powerful forelegs and tough, durable claws, badgers are ridiculously effective diggers. Not only can they burrow through dirt faster than a person using a shovel, but there are reports of badgers digging straight through blacktop and concrete!

7. **Golden poison dart frog**. Native to the Colombian rain forest, this small, brightly colored frog produces an extremely potent poison from glands beneath its skin. Any animal (or person) unlucky enough to get the toxin in its bloodstream faces nearly instant paralysis and then death. Just a few micrograms of golden poison dart frog toxin is enough to kill an adult. It's called a "dart frog" because indigenous peoples have long used the frog's toxic secretions to poison the tips of blow-darts for hunting.

8. **A clam!** An ocean quahog clam, to be precise. In 2006 off the coast of Iceland, a team of researchers captured a quahog that proved to be an incredible 507 years old at the time of its death. (Scientists can count a clam's growth bands to determine its age, similar to counting tree rings.) The clam was playfully nicknamed "Ming," because it was born during the Ming dynasty.

> For a clam that old, you break out the GOOD cocktail sauce.
>
> **CHRIS**

MIGHTY MENACING MERCURY

BY KAREN

When I was maybe five or six, I had a maze toy. It was a clear plastic cube with a maze platform inlay and a bead of mercury. And you were supposed to swirl it around and direct the mercury ball through the maze. That was the first time I had ever seen mercury. What was this wonderful and weird liquid metal thing? It enchanted me.

So of course, after solving the maze, I broke open the cube and got the mercury out and played with it. It was shiny and reflective, and though it was heavy it moved like water. It would separate into little spherical blobs when I squished it with my finger, and I'd watch the microbeads roll along the grooves of my palm.

Like a lot of beautiful things in the world, mercury is very, very, very bad for you. Of course, I didn't learn about this until *after* I'd played with a handful of it. Before the comprehension of modern science, people thought mercury had near-magical qualities. Unfortunately, people throughout history didn't realize until too late that mercury is toxic—and that its toxicity is absorbed through the skin. (Whoops.)

When Qin Shi Huang died, he was touring the country with his retinue. Anxious to keep the emperor's death a secret until they returned home, his advisors kept his body obscured in his private carriage, pretending he was alive for nearly two months (à la *Weekend at Bernie's*) until they reached the palace.

COLIN

THE MERCURY MOTHER LODE IN CHINA

Qin Shi Huang, the first emperor of China, was obsessed with immortality. He drank a lot of "tonics" meant to prolong his life, usually an oddball mix of mercury and other inedible materials such as powdered jade. Despite political scheming and assassination attempts, he most likely died from mercury poisoning—the thing he believed would make him immortal.[11] But even after his death, the mercury obsession lived on. Legends claim that in his elaborate underground mausoleum, court architects built rivers of flowing mercury. Though the tomb hasn't been fully excavated yet to confirm or deny its rumored elaborate mercury construc-

---

11. David Curtis Wright, *The History of China* (Westport, CT: Greenwood Publishing Group, 2001), 49.

GOOD JOB, **BRAIN!**

tions, surrounding soil samples indicate extremely high levels of mercury contamination, according to a 1980s study by the Institute of Geophysical and Geochemical Exploration from the China Institute of Geo-Environment Monitoring.

THE MAD HATTER WASN'T ANGRY

Starting in the 17th century, milliners (hat-makers) used a lot of mercury to make felt hats out of animal hides, often without any safety equipment. The animal skins were rinsed in an orange solution containing mercuric nitrate and this process, known as "carroting," helped separate the fur from the pelt while smoothing the fur. Not only was the solution toxic, but so were its fumes, which caused neurological disorders among the workers of the trade. The neurotoxic effects included irregular heartbeat, uncontrollable shaking, irritability, and, in extreme cases, memory loss and deliriousness. The plight of the hat-maker was so widespread and unfortunately common that it inspired the phrase "mad as a hatter."

Starbucks keeps rejecting my idea for a Mercury Frappuccino.

CHRIS

A SILVER (STOMACH) LINING?

After the Louisiana Purchase in 1803, President Thomas Jefferson appointed Meriwether Lewis and William Clark to explore everything between the Mississippi River and the Pacific Ocean. That swath of wilderness was relatively unknown, and the journey wasn't going to be easy. At the time, there was a lot of pseudo-medical hoopla around bodily fluids like blood and bile, which were believed to be the cause of most diseases. Blood-letting, laxatives, enemas, and vomiting were all acceptable methods of getting rid of disease.

Our expedition boys had a pretty harsh diet out in the wilderness, so they popped mercury chloride pills to ease their constipation. The pills were called "thunderclappers," after the sort of sound effects produced by your buttcheeks. So Lewis and Clark ate mercury and pooped mercury all across America (while probably suffering some degree of poisoning). These mercury laxatives eventually proved handy to historians. Because mercury doesn't break down naturally, modern-day scientists were able to trace Lewis and Clark's path by tracing mercury in the soil.[12] A silver lining, if you will.

---

12. Maurice Possley, "'Thunderbolts' strike twice to mark campsite," *Chicago Tribune,* published July 3, 2005, accessed December 15, 2012, http://articles.chicagotribune.com/2005-07-03/news/0507030260__1__lewis-and-clark-meriwether-lewis-campsite.

ANIMAL SECRETION SPOTLIGHT: BEDTIME BOOGER BUBBLE

BY KAREN

Named for its weird beaky mouth, the funny-looking parrotfish can be found in most tropical waters. But despite its magnificent DayGlo colors, the parrotfish has a not-so-graceful side.

You see, underneath those iridescent scales is fish blood that is irresistible to tiny isopod crustaceans called gnathiids, whose miniature larvae will shimmy into the parrotfish flesh. But the parrotfish has developed a few ways to avoid slowly being eaten alive. During the day, the parrotfish enlists the help of "cleaner fish," who pick out and eat the gnathiid larvae. This symbiotic protection ends, though, when night falls and when most fish go to sleep. So the vulnerable parrotfish has developed a way to protect itself at bedtime.

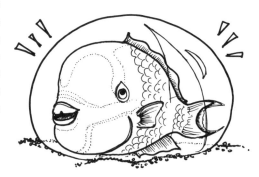

Out comes the booger.

Oh! So much booger.

A polymer-like substance will start oozing out from the fish's face (well, technically from the glands near the gills) until it eventually surrounds the whole fish. Imagine!—blowing a giant snot bubble that covers your whole body, and then sleeping in it! The mucus is clear, and porous enough to let ocean water pass through while keeping the crustaceans out. The whole process actually requires very little energy, so doing this night after night doesn't take a toll on the parrotfish's body. And when morning comes, the fish simply slips out of the mucus and goes about its day. So sweet dreams, parrotfish. May your nights be safe and sound…and snotty.

TUSH TRIVIA

BY DANA

If there's one thing we on *Good Job, Brain!* love talking about, it's poop. If there are several things we love to talk about, one of them would certainly be butt-related trivia. Seriously, the *tuchus* comes up a lot in general conversation. Maybe that happens to you, too? Well, give this quiz on the badonkadonk a shot.

QUESTIONS

1. What butt-related word made the shortlist for Oxford Dictionaries Word of the Year in 2013?

2. According to Sir Mix-A-Lot's 1993 Grammy Award–Winning rap, "Baby Got Back," which fashion magazine has nothing to do with the physical measurements he prefers?

3. Sara Blakely is the inventor of what essential body-shaping garment?

4. Which classic board game was invented by Alfred Mosher Butts in 1938?

5. Which brand of jeans did Oprah appear in and include on her annual Oprah's Favorite Things list for 2004?

6. In Mike Judge's hit TV show *Beavis and Butt-Head*, what color is Butt-head's hair?

7. Which Stevie Nicks single is sampled by Destiny's Child in the song "Bootylicious"?

8. Tucks, Anu-ice, and Res-Q are over-the-counter medications to treat what bodily ailment?

9. The National Football League's Chad Johnson (formerly Chad Ochocinco) was denied a plea bargain judgment for doing what?

10. Which butt-related insult likely dates back to the Middle Ages?

1. **Twerk**. Defined by the *Oxford English Dictionary* as dancing to "popular music in a sexually provocative manner involving thrusting hip movements and a low, squatting stance," it was edged out as the Oxford Dictionaries Word of the Year in 2013 by "selfie."

2. *Cosmopolitan* **magazine**. As Sir Mix-A-Lot raps in "Baby Got Back": "*yeah, baby...when it comes to females,* Cosmo *ain't got nothin' to do with my selection.*"

3. **Spanx**. Blakely wanted the smoothing properties of control top pantyhose without the hassle of the hose. She prototyped it by cutting the legs off some pantyhose, was happy with the results—and the rest is body-shaping history.

4. **Scrabble**. Butts based the game on anagrams and crosswords, popular pastimes in the '20s.

5. **Apple Bottoms Jeans**. Featured on *Oprah* in 2004, these tight pants came from a company cofounded in 2003 by hip-hop star Nelly.

6. **Brown**. Butt-head was the brunet, Beavis the blond. The show *Beavis and Butt-Head* ran on MTV from 1993 to 1997 and was revived for another season in 2011. Huh huh huh.

7. **"Edge of Seventeen."** The popularity of the word "Bootylicious" surged after the 2001 release of this song, and it was added to the *Oxford English Dictionary* in 2004. It's defined as "Esp. of a woman, often with reference to the buttocks: sexually attractive, sexy; shapely."

> "Edge of Seventeen" is actually an eggcorn! Stevie misheard rocker Tom Petty's wife when she said she and Tom met "at the age of seventeen."
>
> **CHRIS**

8. **They are all used to treat hemorrhoids.** One of the ingredients in most hemorrhoid creams is benzocaine, which causes blood vessels to contract, reducing puffiness. Beauty tip #1: you can use hemorrhoid cream on the skin under your eyes to reduce bags and puffiness. Beauty tip #2: using hemorrhoid cream under your eyes regularly can dry out the skin, so only do it before big events like beauty pageants and court dates.

I feel like the makers of Anu-Ice must have chosen literally the first idea they brainstormed for a product name.

COLIN

9. **He got in trouble for slapping his lawyer on the butt.** Chad Johnson was sentenced to 30 days in jail for violating his probation and would have gotten the sentence waived through a plea bargain. When he went to court to get the deal approved by a judge, he playfully slapped his lawyer on the bottom. The judge took offense and rejected the plea deal.

10. **Mooning.** The earliest descriptions of mooning—exposing one's buttocks to an enemy in derision—come from the Middle Ages. The term "mooning," however, was first recorded as college slang in the 1960s.

NOBEL'S SAFETY POWDER

BY COLIN

What comes to mind when you hear the name Alfred Nobel? If you said "the Nobel Peace Prize," congratulations—you're talking out loud to a book. But long before his namesake prize existed, Alfred Nobel made his mark as a pioneer in the field of explosives. In fact, his crowning achievement was one of history's most important inventions. I'm talking of course about…Nobel's Safety Powder. Don't feel bad if you haven't heard of it, because you surely know it as "dynamite."

Now, you may be thinking: "In what way can dynamite be con- 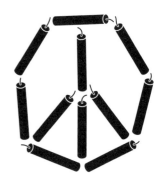sidered *safe*?" And believe me, having grown up on a steady diet of Chuck Jones cartoons, I always equated those iconic red sticks with nothing less than outright mayhem. But in the real world of the 19th century, dynamite was a safety game-changer for industries that rely on explosives, in particular construction and mining. And it all came down to one thing: predictability.

Up until the mid-1800s, the explosive of choice for most uses was good ol' black powder, aka gunpowder. It's relatively safe and fairly easy to make, but it isn't terribly efficient—huge jobs require huge amounts of black powder. In 1847 nitroglycerin was invented, and the clear, heavy liquid proved to be substantially more powerful than traditional black powder. This was great news for people in the business of blowing things up! There was only one problem: it was frighteningly unstable.

Relatively minor shocks or temperature changes could make liquid nitroglycerin explode prematurely, taking with it anyone unfortunate enough to be nearby. To make matters worse, it became increasingly unstable over time. As you can imagine, this was potentially disastrous for crews lugging around glass bottles of the stuff in hot wagons on bumpy roads. Simply manufacturing nitroglycerin was in itself a dicey proposition. Indeed, in 1864 a nitroglycerin blast at a Nobel family–owned explosives factory killed Alfred's younger brother Emil.

Already a talented inventor and successful businessman, Alfred Nobel spent the next few years working on ways to make nitroglycerin safer. In 1867 he finally hit upon the perfect formulation, which we now know as dynamite. Though he really did call it Nobel's Safety Powder in the early days, Nobel also coined its more popular name, inspired by the Greek word *dynamis* ("power").

Dynamite is an elegant solution to a tricky problem: simply put, it's nitroglycerin mixed with an inert porous material, then dried. This retains all the explosion-y goodness of regular liquid nitroglycerin, but in a stabilized form that's more forgiving of shock and heat. The powder gets packed into a simple container—the traditional "red round stick" we know so well from Coyote and Road Runner cartoons—for easy insertion into drill holes. The whole thing is topped off with a blasting cap (like a mini "starter" explosive), which Nobel also invented.

Nobel's breakthrough was an immediate, unqualified success. No longer did workers need to tiptoe around the explosives supply, or pray they didn't drop a jar of liquid nitroglycerin on the way to the blast site. And Alfred Nobel used his business savvy to cash in. Between the factories he owned outright and others that licensed his patents, Nobel sat atop a global dynamite empire. Business was, in every sense, booming.

After Nobel died in 1896, his will revealed his last grand plan. In a complete surprise to his friends and family, Nobel devoted nearly all of his substantial fortune toward establishing the Nobel Foundation. He left detailed instructions for what would become known as the Nobel Prizes—originally, five awards for Chemistry, Physics, Literature, Physiology/Medicine, and, of course, Peace. Aside from a few tweaks here and there over the past century-plus, the Nobel Prizes today are largely the same as they were in the inaugural year of 1901. And sure enough, when you hear "Nobel," the odds are you think "peace" and not "kaboom!"

SO IT'S COME TO THIS: A PAGE ABOUT BOOGERS

BY CHRIS

⚜

Finally!

DANA

Boogers are great. You might not like them, but if all the boogers in the world were to disappear, we'd all be dead. Boogers save your life, on a regular basis. When you breathe in, which is important for living, you're not just taking in glorious life-giving oxygen. You're also pulling up any bacteria, viruses, microbes, very small rocks, and what-have-you that might be floating in the air. The mucus in your nasal cavities is really good at grabbing this stuff. Cilia, the tiny hairs in your nose, constantly move the mucus back into your esophagus. Your body is constantly generating more mucus to suck up more garbage, and you swallow it constantly. Folks, you are drinking a refreshing quart of mucus a day.

Anyway, we're not talking about mucus *per se*. We're talking about boogers. I keep saying this because there is no specific scientific term for them. They're just dried mucus. The mucus that gets close to the edge of your nose loses its gooey moisture, airs out, and becomes a booger.

What you do with it after that is your own business. We're not here to judge. It is said that King Tutankhamun had his own personal nose-picker. The rest of us have to rely on self-service. One 1995 study in the *Journal of Clinical Psychiatry* found that 91 percent of people—responding anonymously, via the mail—picked their noses.[13] That's who *admitted* it, mind you. This study went on to discuss the rare cases in which nose-picking went from "[some]thing everyone does" to "dangerous." When does it cross the line into *rhinotillexomania*—from the Latin words for "nose," "pick at," and "compulsive"?

Of the 244 people who responded to that survey, two said they'd picked their nose so much that they'd perforated their septum. Folks, serious talk time here: if you poke a hole through from one nostril to the other, it is *time to get help*.

---

13. J. W. Jefferson and T. D. Thompson, "Rhinotillexomania: psychiatric disorder or habit?" *Journal of Clinical Psychiatry* 56, no. 2 (February 1995): 56–9.

GOOD JOB, **BRAIN!**

(MOSTLY) CUTE BABY ANIMALS

BY DANA

⸙

When I'm feeling stressed, nothing makes me feel better faster than a picture of a cute baby animal. That face! That clumsy baby walk! Mmm...just thinking about it makes me feel calmer. You might want to take a look at a picture of a baby animal before you take this quiz, because it's a little tricky. Your job is to match the baby names with the species. The hard part is that some of these animals have multiple names for their young. You must figure out which one name applies to *all* the animals in that grouping.

BABY NAMES

1. ____ Calf
2. ____ Cria
3. ____ Cub
4. ____ Foal
5. ____ Hatchling
6. ____ Joey
7. ____ Kit
8. ____ Larva
9. ____ Nymph
10. ____ Shoat
11. ____ Poult
12. ____ Puggle
13. ____ Pup
14. ____ Whelp

ANIMALS

A. Alpaca, llama
B. Anteater, armadillo, bat
C. Boar, hog, pig
D. Cockroach, grasshopper, cicada
E. Crocodile, turtle, dinosaur
F. Echidna, platypus
G. Eel, clam, yellow jacket
H. Elephant, giraffe, manatee
I. Fox, skunk, weasel
J. Opossum, wallaby, koala
K. Otter, tiger, wolf
L. Raccoon, walrus, bear
M. Turkey, grouse
N. Zebra, donkey, mule

1. **H.** Elephant, giraffe, manatee (Calf)

2. **A.** Alpaca, llama (Cria)

3. **L.** Racoon, walrus, bear (Cub)

4. **N.** Zebra, donkey, mule (Foal)

5. **E.** Crocodile, turtle, dinosaur (Hatchling)

6. **J.** Opossum, wallaby, koala (Joey)

7. **I.** Fox, skunk, weasel (Kit)

8. **G.** Eel, clam, yellow jacket (Larva)

9. **D.** Cockroach, grasshopper, cicada (Nymph)

10. **C.** Boar, hog, pig (Shoat)

11. **M.** Turkey, grouse (Poult)

12. **F.** Echidna, platypus (Puggle)

13. **B.** Anteater, armadillo, bat (Pup)

14. **K.** Otter, tiger, wolf (Whelp)

LIKE AN ANIMAL!

BY COLIN

If I said you exhibited *feline* grace or *canine* loyalty, you'd probably be flattered. But what if I said you had a *vulpine* face, or a *caprine* odor? Don't sweat it if you're confused—this matching quiz will help you decide whether to be delighted or offended!

Match up the "-ine" adjectives with the appropriate animals.

ADJECTIVES

1. ____ Canine
2. ____ Feline
3. ____ Bovine
4. ____ Equine
5. ____ Ursine
6. ____ Lupine
7. ____ Porcine
8. ____ Ovine
9. ____ Piscine
10. ____ Vulpine
11. ____ Caprine
12. ____ Lacertine
13. ____ Murine
14. ____ Ranine
15. ____ Asinine

ANIMALS

A. Fish
B. Horse
C. Mouse
D. Bear
E. Lizard
F. Dog
G. Pig
H. Frog
I. Fox
J. Donkey
K. Goat
L. Cat
M. Sheep
N. Wolf
O. Cow

1. **F.** Dog (Canine)

2. **L.** Cat (Feline)

3. **O.** Cow (Bovine—also applies to bulls and oxes)

4. **B.** Horse (Equine)

5. **D.** Bear (Ursine)

6. **N.** Wolf (Lupine)

7. **G.** Pig (Porcine)

8. **M.** Sheep (Ovine)

9. **A.** Fish (Piscine)

10. **I.** Fox (Vulpine)

11. **K.** Goat (Caprine)

12. **E.** Lizard (Lacertine)

13. **C.** Mouse (Murine)

14. **H.** Frog (Ranine)

15. **J.** Donkey (Asinine)

Now that you have the knowledge of animal adjectives on your side, be sure to use your powers only for good! (Oh, and I apologize for implying you smell like a goat.)

THE CENTAUR OF ATTENTION

BY KAREN

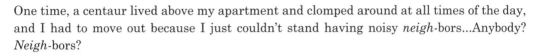

One time, a centaur lived above my apartment and clomped around at all times of the day, and I had to move out because I just couldn't stand having noisy *neigh*-bors...Anybody? *Neigh*-bors?

So here's your unofficial guide to all the different types of equine-human mash-ups in Ancient Greek mythology!

CENTAUR

Ah, let's start with the basics. You've seen them gallivanting in the forests near Hogwarts or roaming in the fields of Narnia. The classic half-human, half-horse creature is a centaur; with a horse body, four horse legs, and a male torso (usually time super-ripped) and head. Currently the most popular belief is that the idea of the centaur stemmed from the initial reaction of cultures seeing people riding horses for the first time; how majestic and almost magical it must have seemed! And important to note: centaurs are specifically dudes. Female variants are called "centaurides."

SATYR

The satyr to me is like Diet Centaur: instead of a full horse body, a satyr has a human torso but only two equine legs. Also, satyrs aren't specifically part horse: some variants (including Roman satyrs) are more goat-like. Often you'll see satyrs depicted as spirited frolickers while playing a flute and palling around with the Greek god of pleasure, Dionysus.

ONOCENTAUR

Oh, no centaur. I'm part donkey. On one end of the equine-human mash-up spectrum you have the majestic centaur; on the other end you get your stubborn donkey dude. Replace the centaur's horse part with the stubborn donkey and you've got your onocentaur, a creature who has a rational human brain but a terribly wild and temperamental body. Probably doesn't smell good, either.

ICHTHYOCENTAUR

And now it gets weird. If you're familiar with Greek word roots, then you'd probably guess that the name breaks down to "fish horse man," and you'd be 100 percent correct. Replace the hind legs and butt of a centaur with a humongous fish tail, and you've got yourself an ichthyocentaur. The two main ichthyocentaurs are brothers Bythos and Aphros, who—unlike most centaur creatures—are pretty peaceful and prefer chilling in the ocean. But take out the human part of the equation and you have a "hippocamp," a mythological creature that's a horse with a fishtail, often seen dragging Poseidon's lazy butt around. A literal sea horse!

WHO, WHAT, AND WHERE

THE EARTH IS FULL OF FASCINATING PEOPLE, THINGS, PLACES.

COME ALONG WITH US ON A TRIP AROUND THE WORLD!

OFFICIAL STATE WHATEVERS

BY CHRIS

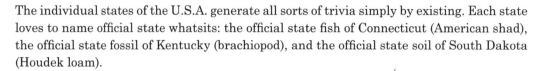

The individual states of the U.S.A. generate all sorts of trivia simply by existing. Each state loves to name official state whatsits: the official state fish of Connecticut (American shad), the official state fossil of Kentucky (brachiopod), and the official state soil of South Dakota (Houdek loam).

I know what you're thinking, and no, as of the writing of this book, Connecticut does not have an official state soil, but everybody is pulling for Windsor soil to take that one home.

I don't expect you to be able to guess things like the official state flying mammal of Oklahoma (the Mexican free-tailed bat), but here are some state symbols I think you might be able to come up with, since they all make (some degree of) sense.

CLUES

1. This is the official state cookie of Pennsylvania.

2. Both Massachusetts and Louisiana have official state donuts. What are they?

3. What 1964 recording by The McCoys, a staple at Ohio sporting events, is the state's official rock song?

4. This state's official state drink is "coffee milk."

5. Ice cream is the official state dessert of Virginia, but what state's official dessert is the ice cream *cone*?

6. The Boston Terrier is the official state dog of Massachusetts; the Alaskan Malamute is Alaska's. What state's official dog is the Chesapeake Bay Retriever?

7. What drink, originally called Fruit Smack, was invented in and is now the official state soft drink of Nebraska?

8. In New York, it's "Apple." In Minnesota and Virginia, it's "Blueberry." In Massachusetts it's "Corn," and in Hawaii it's "Coconut." I'm describing their official state...*what*?

9. In 2005, North Carolina declared this to be the official state carnivorous plant.

10. New Mexico has an official state question—"Red or green?" To what does this refer?

11. Every state has some sort of official food, but this is the only state with an official state *flavor*.

1. **Chocolate chip cookie**, probably made with chocolate from Hershey, PA.

2. **Boston cream** and beignet, respectively.

3. **"Hang On Sloopy."** I'm sure you Buckeyes knew that one.

4. **Rhode Island**. It's like chocolate milk, but with coffee-flavored syrup.

5. **Missouri**. The ice cream cone was, famously, invented at the St. Louis World's Fair in 1904.

6. **Chesapeake Bay Retriever**. Maryland named it the state dog in 1964.

7. **Kool-Aid**, created by Edwin Perkins in the 1920s.

8. **Muffins**, because, yes, official state muffins are a thing.

9. **The Venus flytrap**, so rare that you could end up in prison for picking one of them.[14]

10. **Chile**. "Red or green?" is a question asked at restaurants about which pepper or sauce the customer would like.

11. **Vermont**. The flavor, naturally, is maple.

---

14. John R. Platt, "Venus Fly Traps Risk Extinction in the Wild at the Hands of Poachers," *Scientific American*, published January 22, 2015, accessed July 20, 2016, http://blogs.scientificamerican.com/extinction-countdown/venus-flytraps-risk-extinction-in-the-wild-at-the-hands-of-poachers.

BRAD PITT OR LASERS?

BY COLIN

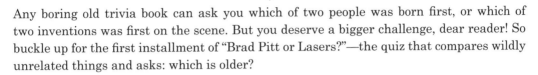

Any boring old trivia book can ask you which of two people was born first, or which of two inventions was first on the scene. But you deserve a bigger challenge, dear reader! So buckle up for the first installment of "Brad Pitt or Lasers?"—the quiz that compares wildly unrelated things and asks: which is older?

(For a person, this means the year he or she was born; for a landmark, it means the year construction was completed; for a book, movie, TV show, or product, it means the year it was released.)

QUESTIONS

1. Which is older: **Brad Pitt** or **lasers**?

2. Which is older: the **saxophone** or **toilet paper**?

3. Which is older: *Alice's Adventures in Wonderland* or **Levi's jeans**?

4. Which is older: the **Brooklyn Bridge** or **Budweiser beer**?

5. Which is older: **Betty White** or **penicillin**?

6. Which is older: **bubble gum** or **Trojan condoms**?

7. Which is older: **Oreo cookies** or the **Volkswagen Beetle**?

8. Which is older: the **Barbie doll** or the **New York Mets**?

1. **Lasers** are older than Brad Pitt. The first functioning laser was fired in 1960; actor Brad Pitt was born in 1963.

2. The **saxophone** is older than toilet paper. Belgian inventor and musician Adolphe Sax patented the saxophone in 1846; the first commercial toilet paper was introduced in 1857.

3. *Alice's Adventures in Wonderland* is older than Levi's jeans. Lewis Carroll published *Alice's Adventures in Wonderland* in 1865; Levi Strauss and partner Jacob Davis patented their blue jeans in 1873.

4. **Budweiser beer** is older than the Brooklyn Bridge. Anheuser-Busch introduced Budweiser in 1876; the Brooklyn Bridge was completed in 1883.

5. **Betty White** is older than penicillin. Actress Betty White was born in 1922; penicillin was discovered in 1928 by Sir Alexander Fleming.

> OMG Betty White. This is amazing.
>
> **KAREN**

6. **Trojan condoms** are older than bubble gum. Trojan condoms were introduced in 1916; Fleer introduced Dubble Bubble, the first bubble gum, in 1928.

7. **Oreo cookies** are older than the VW Beetle. Nabisco introduced Oreo cookies in 1912; Volkswagen produced its first Beetle (initially called the Type 1) in 1938.

8. The **Barbie doll** is older than the New York Mets. Mattel introduced Barbie in 1959; the New York Mets played their first season in 1962.

SETTING SAIL ON THE GARBAGE SHIP

BY CHRIS

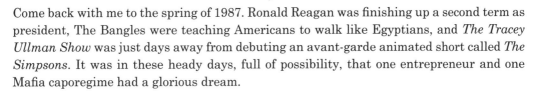

Come back with me to the spring of 1987. Ronald Reagan was finishing up a second term as president, The Bangles were teaching Americans to walk like Egyptians, and *The Tracey Ullman Show* was just days away from debuting an avant-garde animated short called *The Simpsons*. It was in these heady days, full of possibility, that one entrepreneur and one Mafia caporegime had a glorious dream.

That dream involved garbage.

Specifically, New York garbage, with which the city was and continues to be blessed in abundance. Our plucky heroes learned that the great state of North Carolina would pay them $5 a ton for garbage. Why would anyone do that? Well, they were setting up a pilot program to turn garbage into methane for energy. They'd set up a landfill in such a way that within a couple of years they'd be collecting valuable gas.

Learning of this lucrative refuse opportunity, businessman Lowell Harrelson teamed up with Salvatore Avellino—who was in the "waste disposal business" in approximately the same way that Tony Soprano was—to pile 3,000 tons of the Big Apple's finest garbage onto a barge called the *Mobro 4000* and ship it down the coast to North Carolina, where it would surely be given a hero's welcome.

What actually happened was that the barge—and you really could tell, just by glancing at it, that it was a massive pile of fetid trash—caught the eye of a local news crew once it got to North Carolina. They ran with the somewhat-but-not-entirely-accurate story that New York was looking to pawn off its garbage onto the good people of North Carolina. Now facing a public outcry, North Carolina officials put the kibosh on the deal, telling the garbage to hit the bricks.

Undeterred, and with an impressive can-do attitude, Harrelson and Avellino continued to send their shipload of trash down the eastern seaboard of the United States. They tried to dump it in Louisiana, but the *Mobro*, which had been out on the water for weeks, was turned away there, too. It was now a national story, spiced up with the allegation that the *Mobro* might be carrying infectious, dangerous waste. Now *nobody* wanted it. They headed on down the Gulf Coast to Mexico, they went to Belize, they tried Florida. No, no, no. This garbage was now more well-traveled than most actual residents of New York City.

There's a myth that started up when the *Mobro* was making its voyage: that its inability to return to shore meant that America had "run out of space" to put its landfill garbage. This wasn't actually true, but the *Mobro* incident is now seen as a catalyst for the recycling movement in the late 1980s.

Mobro 4000? Too obvious. Should have called it the *Mafiyacht.*

DANA

Having become an international laughingstock, the *Mobro* finally got an inspection from the Environmental Protection Agency, two months after it had left New York. There was nothing hazardous on board, the EPA found. The *Mobro* returned to New York and sat there for a while before its precious load was finally incinerated in Brooklyn.

The *New York Times* estimated that Lowell Harrelson had lost about one million dollars on the venture.

BELGIUM OR NOT BELGIUM?

BY DANA

When we were raising funds to start the *Good Job, Brain!* podcast, we promised to make a show centered on our top Kickstarter backer. That winning backer was Fred, an extremely chill video game and Tarantino enthusiast from Belgium. For our "Fred" show, I made a quiz called "Belgium or Not Belgium?" All Karen, Colin, and Chris had to do was determine whether a particular fact was true about Belgium or somewhere other than Belgium. We discovered that unless you're from there, it's a lot harder than you'd think. Now it's your turn to try, so finish eating your Belgian waffle (Belgium), strap on your lederhosen (Not Belgium), and get ready to play *Good Job, Brain!*'s favorite Belgium-related trivia game!

QUESTIONS

Are these things true about Belgium or Not Belgium?

1. Brussels sprouts are from here.

2. There are three official languages here.

3. The coffee filter was invented here.

4. This country has the most ski resorts of any nation.

5. The metric system was invented here.

6. There are more comics-makers per capita here than anywhere else in the world.

7. *The Communist Manifesto* was written here.

8. This is the least-populated country in the European Union.

9. Jean-Claude Van Damme is from here.

10. Christoph Waltz was born here.

11. Audrey Hepburn was born here.

12. This country has Europe's largest economy.

13. The parachute was invented here.

14. Its flag has black, yellow, and red horizontal stripes.

15. The largest diamond district in the world is in this country.

1. **Belgium**. Brussels sprouts, as we know them now, might have been grown here as early as the 13th century!

2. **Belgium**. The three official languages are Flemish, French, and German.

3. **Not Belgium**. The coffee filter was invented in Germany.

4. **Not Belgium**. The United States has by far the most ski resorts.

5. **Not Belgium**. The metric system was invented in France.

6. **Belgium!** Belgium has more comics-makers per capita than anywhere else in the world. Both *Tintin* and *The Smurfs* were created in Belgium.

7. **Belgium**. *The Communist Manifesto* was written in Brussels by Karl Marx in 1848.

8. **Not Belgium**. Of the 28 members of the European Union, Belgium is the ninth most populated, with 11.3 million people. Malta is the least populated, with 430,000 people.

9. **Belgium**. Jean Claude Van Damme, "The Muscles from Brussels," is a proud son of Belgium.

10. **Not Belgium**. Academy Award–winning actor Christoph Waltz was born in Austria to German parents.

11. **Belgium**. Yes, Audrey Hepburn was born in Belgium to British and Dutch parents.

12. **Not Belgium**. Germany has Europe's largest economy.

13. **Not Belgium**. The modern parachute was invented in France in the late 18th century by Louis-Sébastien Lenormand, who also coined the word.

14. **Not Belgium**. The Belgian flag has black, yellow, and red vertical stripes. The German flag has black, yellow, and red horizontal stripes.

15. **Belgium**. More than 80 percent of the world's rough diamonds pass through Antwerp, Belgium.

SOUNDS LIKE A CAPITAL IDEA!

BY KAREN

Of the nearly 200 world capitals, a fair few of them are homophones of words or phrases in the English language. (Some of them are a little weird, because I made them up.) The answers to these clues will sound quite a bit like capital cities you may have heard of!

Here's an example:

Clue: *Aretha Franklin and James Brown have it.*

Answer: *Soul = Seoul, South Korea*

CLUES

1. A common buffalo activity.

2. Sandwich place that just opened.

3. Greek letters for X and R.

4. Half of quadruplin'.

5. A workaholic, competitive personality.

6. Nirvana-achieving mosquito?

7. Lion-O's hairstyle?

See if you can come up with your own capital homophones!

> I'm guessing #6 is not Quito (Ecuador), the super-chill mosquito?
>
> **DANA**

1. Roam = Rome, Italy

2. New deli = New Delhi, India

3. Chi Rho = Cairo, Egypt

4. Doublin' = Dublin, Ireland

5. Type A = Taipei, Taiwan

6. Buddha Pest = Budapest, Hungary

7. Cat-man 'do = Kathmandu, Nepal

BUTT IS IT ART?

BY CHRIS

The particulars are long lost to history, but we do know this: at some point around the first century BC, a Roman sculptor created a marble statue of a woman. Maybe she was Venus, goddess of love. Maybe he was copying a Greek bronze of Aphrodite from hundreds of years prior. Who knows? Anyway, the thing about this statue is that the woman in question was holding up her skirt in such a way that you could see her butt.

The statue was lost for centuries, and when it was discovered again in Rome around the 16th century it was a little worse for the wear. It was missing the head, as often happens. And one of the arms…and one of the legs. In fact, at that point, it was pretty much just a butt.

But it was a good-looking rear end, so beautiful that it inspired the 16th-century artist who restored the statue to add what you might call a bit of *editorial commentary*. The head he added was turned facing over the shoulder so that Venus was looking back on her own behind. With an expression on her face suggesting, "Damn, do I have a great butt."

And so was born the very famous work of art known as the Venus Callipyge or Callipygian Venus. That's from the Greek words *kallos* ("beauty") and *pyge* ("buttocks"), and it means what you think it does.

DAYUM!

We don't know where the head was facing on the original, but it was the addition of the head-turn that made this statue so fascinating, so inviting of interpretation. Like the Mona Lisa's enigmatic half-smile, but looking at a butt.

A 19th-century guide titled *The Royal Museum at Naples: Being Some Account of the Erotic Paintings, Bronzes, and Statues Contained in That Famous "Cabinet Secret"* said that the statue "is placed in a reserved hall, where the curious are only introduced under the surveillance of a guardian, though even this precaution has not prevented the rounded forms which won for the goddess the name of Callipyge, from being covered with a dark tint, which betrays the profane kisses that fanatic admirers have every day impressed there."

That's right—crazy people kissed the statue's butt so much that it discolored the marble. You can see the Callipygian Venus (but please do not kiss it) in the Naples National Archaeological Museum in Naples, Italy.

I'm curious how many people have completed the Blarney Stone/ Callipygian Venus kissing twofer!

COLIN

LICENSE TO QUIZ

BY COLIN

Get ready for a road trip! Yes, that classic American vacation, in which the thrill of the voyage can easily wear off 30 minutes into a hot car ride. So we're going to pass the time with a twist on the classic License Plate Game: I'll give you several license plate slogans from all over the U.S.A., and you tell me where they're from.

> If you get any wrong, we get to slug you in the shoulder.
>
> **CHRIS**

SLOGANS

1. Sunshine State

2. Famous Potatoes

3. Land of Lincoln

4. The Silver State

5. Great Faces. Great Places.

6. Evergreen State

7. Land of Enchantment

8. Live Free or Die

9. Taxation without Representation

10. Birthplace of Aviation

1. **Florida**. Did you know that Florida leads the nation in alligator-related deaths? I'd probably opt to focus on the sunshine, too.

2. **Idaho**. This slogan is a show of respect for the state's most important cash crop.

3. **Illinois**. Although he was born in Kentucky, Abraham Lincoln served in the Illinois state legislature and represented Illinois in Congress before becoming the 16th President of the United States.

4. **Nevada**. This is Nevada's official nickname, a nod to the importance of silver mining in state history.

5. **South Dakota**. "Great Faces" refers to the presidential faces on Mount Rushmore, South Dakota's most popular tourist attraction.

6. **Washington**. It's safe to say there's no shortage of pine, spruce, and Douglas-fir trees in Washington. (Seriously, they've got it covered.)

7. **New Mexico**. This charmingly earnest slogan has graced New Mexico license plates for more than 75 years. In 1999 it became the official state nickname.

8. **New Hampshire**. New Hampshire proudly embraces this brash motto, which epitomizes the state's fierce independent spirit. (As George Carlin once noted, "Live Free or Die" is about as far as you can get from "Famous Potatoes.")

> New Hampshire is the only state without seat belt laws for adults, so it's both Living Free *and* Dying.
>
> **DANA**

9. **Washington, DC.** This is a rather pointed reference to the fact that DC residents pay federal taxes, yet have no voting representation in Congress.

10. **Ohio**. This is a tricky one! Both Ohio and North Carolina can lay claim to the enduring legacy of the Wright brothers: Orville and Wilbur Wright were longtime residents of Dayton, Ohio, but their famous airplane demonstration took place near Kitty Hawk, North Carolina. (Indeed, the license plate slogan for North Carolina is "First in Flight.")

BRAD PITT OR LASERS? PART II

BY COLIN

It's time for another round of "Brad Pitt or Lasers?," the quiz that tests your date-ability! I've prepared a new list of totally unrelated things, and once again it's your job to answer: which is older?

(For a person, this means the year he or she was born; for a landmark, it means the year construction was completed; for a movie, TV show, or product, it means the year it was released.)

QUESTIONS

1. Which is older: **Oprah Winfrey** or the **Ford Mustang**?

2. Which is older: **Coca-Cola** or the **Eiffel Tower**?

3. Which is older: the **electric guitar** or the **Golden Gate Bridge**?

4. Which is older: **Donald Trump** or **Mr. Potato Head**?

5. Which is older: **basketball** or the **spring-loaded mousetrap**?

6. Which is older: **Vaseline** or the **flashlight**?

7. Which is older: **MTV** or *Tetris*?

8. Which is older: *Batman* or *The Hobbit*?

Answers

1. **Oprah Winfrey** is older than the Ford Mustang. TV host and media mogul Oprah Winfrey was born in 1954; the Ford Motor Company rolled out the first-generation Mustang in 1964.

2. **Coca-Cola** is older than the Eiffel Tower. Pharmacist John Pemberton created Coca-Cola in 1886 in Atlanta, Georgia; the Eiffel Tower opened to the public during the 1889 Exposition Universelle (world's fair) in—where else?—Paris, France.

3. The **electric guitar** is older than the Golden Gate Bridge. The Ro-Pat-In Company introduced the solid-body electric guitar in 1931; San Francisco's iconic Golden Gate Bridge opened to the public in 1937.

4. **Donald Trump** is older than Mr. Potato Head. Businessman, politician, and noted loud talker Donald Trump was born in 1946; the Hasbro toy company introduced Mr. Potato Head in 1952.

5. **Basketball** is older than the spring-loaded mousetrap. James Naismith devised the rules for basketball in 1891 while teaching physical education in Springfield, Massachusetts; the classic swing-bar mousetrap was patented in 1894 by William C. Hooker (followed closely by several similar devices).

6. **Vaseline** is older than the flashlight. Chemist Robert Chesebrough began selling refined petroleum jelly under the brand name Vaseline in 1872; the modern electric flashlight was patented in 1899 by British inventor David Misell.

7. **MTV** is older than *Tetris*. MTV broadcast its first music video ("Video Killed the Radio Star" by the Buggles) in 1981; the classic video game *Tetris* was created in 1984 by programmer Alexey Pajitnov.

8. *The Hobbit* is older than Batman. J.R.R. Tolkien's best-selling fantasy novel *The Hobbit* was published in 1937; Batman first appeared in the pages of *Detective Comics* #27, released in May 1939.

OMGEOGRAPHY!

BY COLIN

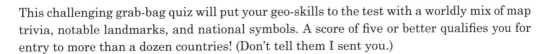

This challenging grab-bag quiz will put your geo-skills to the test with a worldly mix of map trivia, notable landmarks, and national symbols. A score of five or better qualifies you for entry to more than a dozen countries! (Don't tell them I sent you.)

QUESTIONS

1. What country has the longest coastline in the world?

2. California is home to the lowest surface elevation in the United States: Badwater Basin in Death Valley, at 282 feet below sea level. Which state has the highest surface elevation?

3. What is the largest lake in Africa?

4. How many time zones are there in China?

5. Mount Everest is the highest mountain on Earth, and any pub quiz team worth its salt knows K2 is the second highest. But what does the K in K2 stand for?

6. The city in Russia that we now call St. Petersburg was originally named...St. Petersburg. Between then and now, however, it had two other official names. Name either one.

7. What is the only country that doesn't have a rectangular (including square) national flag?

8. What's the first country to ring in the new year every January 1 (and the first to experience each new day)?

1. **Canada**. Although it's difficult to determine the exact length of any country's coastline, Canada is so far ahead of everyone else that quibbles over precision are irrelevant. By even the most conservative estimate, Canada has more than 125,000 miles of coastline!

2. **Alaska**. At 20,310 feet, the peak of Denali (formerly known as Mount McKinley) marks the highest elevation in the United States. In the 48 contiguous states, the highest point is the peak of California's Mount Whitney, at 14,505 feet. (Coincidentally, Mount Whitney is a mere 85 miles from Badwater Basin in Death Valley.)

3. **Lake Victoria**. The largest of the African Great Lakes, Lake Victoria borders Tanzania, Uganda, and Kenya. It's the second-largest freshwater lake in the world by surface area, behind only Lake Superior in North America.

4. **One time zone**. Sorry, this is sort of a trick question. After the Communist Party assumed power in 1949, all of China was standardized to a single time zone, ostensibly in the name of national unity. (Prior to that, there were five time zones.) France has 12 time zones, the most of any country, thanks to far-flung dependent territories such as French Polynesia and Martinique. (In terms of contiguous time zones, Russia has the most, with 11.)

5. **Karakoram**. K2 was the second mountain surveyed in the Karakoram Range, which covers parts of China, India, and Pakistan. Peaks were given numeric designations in the order they were mapped, although local names took precedence for most of them—for example, K1 kept its traditional name, Masherbrum. Since K2 didn't appear to have a local name, the survey designation stuck as its primary name.

6. **Petrograd and Leningrad**. The fickle city's naming history is as follows:

1703—founded as St. Petersburg

1914—renamed Petrograd

1924—renamed Leningrad

1991—renamed St. Petersburg

7. **Nepal**. The Nepalese national flag is composed of two stacked triangular shapes, as shown here. (The flag's actual colors are red and white, with a blue border.)

8. **Kiribati** (pronounced "Kiribas" by locals). The International Date Line loops around this tiny island nation in the Pacific Ocean, putting it in the "furthest-ahead" time zone possible (UTC+14). Due to this quirk in the path of the Date Line, Hawaii is a day behind Kiribati time-wise, despite lying directly to the north.

PROVINCES, EH?

BY CHRIS

❦

One of the worst, most mean-spirited teachers I ever had once berated an entire fifth-grade social studies class for not being able to name, apropos of absolutely nothing, the 10 Canadian provinces. "All Canadian children can recite all 50 United States," she spat at us. Later in life, I interrogated some Canadians and found this to be patently untrue.

Years later, with the perspective granted to me as an adult, I realized something important about that day: some teachers are just total b-holes. Even so, upon joining a pub quiz team, I quickly learned that knowing the 10 Canadian provinces would be pretty helpful for scoring a few points. Here's a fantastic mnemonic we heard, and never forgot:

Billy

And

Sally

Made

Our

Queen

Nervous

Playing

Near

Needles

GOOD JOB, **BRAIN!**

This is an image that really sticks in your head, right? Look at the Queen, she's so scandalized! The first letters of each word in the sentence indicate the 10 Canadian provinces, from west to east:

- British Columbia
- Alberta
- Saskatchewan
- Manitoba
- Ontario
- Quebec
- New Brunswick
- Prince Edward Island
- Nova Scotia
- Newfoundland

Yeah, it gets a little sketchy toward the end there, since Prince Edward Island and all the "N" provinces are kind of smashed up into each other. But this'll get you 95 percent of the way there.

Also note the Queen screaming "You're Not Nice!" at poor Billy and Sally. That's a mini-mnemonic for the three Canadian territories:

- Yukon
- Northwest Territories
- Nunavut

(If that doesn't work for you, just picture Ygritte from *Game of Thrones* saying, "You know nothing, Jon Snow." It's almost as cold beyond the Wall as it is in Canada.)

CATCH OF THE DAY

BY DANA

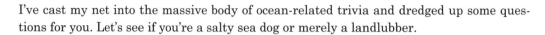

I've cast my net into the massive body of ocean-related trivia and dredged up some questions for you. Let's see if you're a salty sea dog or merely a landlubber.

QUESTIONS

1. About how deep is the ocean at its deepest point?
     a. 18,000 feet
     b. 26,000 feet
     c. 36,000 feet
     d. 42,000 feet

2. SpongeBob SquarePants makes his home below which Pacific atoll?
     a. Loyalty Island
     b. Wreck Reef
     c. Bikini Atoll
     d. Spratly Island

3. In Lewis Carroll's poem "The Walrus and the Carpenter," which sea creatures are tricked into taking a walk along the beach?
     a. Salmon
     b. Crabs
     c. Oysters
     d. Porpoises

4. Was "Yo Ho (A Pirate's Life for Me)" written for Disney or Not Disney?

   a. Disney

   b. Not Disney

5. What phrase is a euphemism for the bottom of the ocean, where shipwrecks and dead sailors reside?

   a. Jolly Roger

   b. Fiddler's Green

   c. Davy Jones' Locker

   d. Dead Man's Chest

6. St. Elmo's Fire was named for St. Erasmus, the patron saint of sailors. Besides being the name of a 1985 Brat Pack movie, what is St. Elmo's Fire?

   a. Gastrointestinal distress commonly experienced by people new to sailing

   b. A rare STD

   c. A weather phenomenon

   d. Both A and B

7. Naturally occurring pearls are usually formed around:

   a. Sand

   b. Baby oysters

   c. Parasites

   d. Mermaid tears

8. On a boat, "starboard" is:

   a. The front

   b. The back

   c. The right

   d. The left

1. **(c) About 36,000 feet**. As far as we know, the deepest part is the Challenger Deep, located in the southern part of the Mariana Trench in the Pacific Ocean. It was discovered in 1875 on a scientific expedition by the ship HMS *Challenger*. The average depth of the ocean is about 12,100 feet.

2. **(c) Bikini Atoll**. SpongeBob lives in Bikini Bottom, which show creator Stephen Hillenburg confirmed is below Bikini Atoll in the Pacific Ocean. Bikini Atoll is part of the Marshall Islands and was where the U.S. detonated 23 nuclear devices between 1946 and 1958. It's possible the nuclear testing may have something to do with why the marine life in that part of the ocean started talking and wearing pants.

3. **(c) Oysters**. The poem about the doomed spats (baby oysters) is recited by Tweedledee and Tweedledum to Alice in *Through the Looking Glass*.

4. **(a) Disney**. "Yo Ho (A Pirate's Life for Me)" was written by George Bruns and Xavier Atencio for the Pirates of the Caribbean ride at Disney theme parks. It was, however, loosely based on the sea shanty "Dead Man's Chest," which Robert Louis Stevenson wrote for *Treasure Island* (1883).

5. **(c) Davy Jones' Locker** is the place at the bottom of the ocean where dead sailors reside. The Jolly Roger is the name of the skull-and-crossbones pirate ship flag. Fiddler's Green is the afterlife for sailors who served more than 50 years, and where people dance, drink, and listen to nonstop fiddling. Dead Man's Chest is both the name of the sea shanty in *Treasure Island* and the name of the second film in the *Pirates of the Caribbean* franchise.

6. **(c) St. Elmo's Fire** is a weather phenomenon that occurs occasionally during thunderstorms. As a ship's mast cuts through an electric field in the atmosphere, luminous plasma that looks like blue flames sometimes appears on the mast. Even though it looks pretty freaky (Ahh! Ghost fire!), historically St. Elmo's

Fire was seen as a good omen because it often happened near the end of a thunderstorm.

7. **(c) Parasites**. Contrary to popular belief, natural pearls are only rarely formed around sand. Bivalve mollusks such as oysters and mussels are *fantastic* at removing sand from their shells. It's much more common that a worm, or sometimes a tiny fish or snail, makes its way inside the shell and latches onto the flesh. Unable to get rid of the parasite, the mollusk secretes a substance called "nacre," which encases the intruder. Over time, with many layers of nacre produced, a pearl is formed. In fact, when holes are added to natural pearls for jewelry-making, a liquid often oozes out—the decomposed parasite.[15]

8. **(c) Starboard** is the right side of a boat. The word comes from Old English *stéorbord*, meaning the side of the ship with the steering paddle. Most ships today don't have steering paddles, so the literal translation has gotten separated from what we might commonly see on boats. For some help remembering that starboard is on the right, try this: "star light, star bright, starboard is on the right." (And if you're wondering, the left side is called "port.")

---

15. "Ten Things You Didn't Know about Pearls," Pearls.com, published August 29, 2014, accessed July 20, 2016, www.pearls.com/blogs/news/15236297-ten-things-you-didnt-know-about-pearls.

THE TRUTH ABOUT BURIED TREASURE

BY COLIN

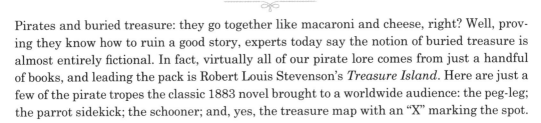

Pirates and buried treasure: they go together like macaroni and cheese, right? Well, proving they know how to ruin a good story, experts today say the notion of buried treasure is almost entirely fictional. In fact, virtually all of our pirate lore comes from just a handful of books, and leading the pack is Robert Louis Stevenson's *Treasure Island*. Here are just a few of the pirate tropes the classic 1883 novel brought to a worldwide audience: the peg-leg; the parrot sidekick; the schooner; and, yes, the treasure map with an "X" marking the spot.

For his part, Stevenson was inspired by a variety of sources, including Washington Irving's *Tales of a Traveller*, which included a heavy dose of treasure hunting, and Edgar Allan Poe's *The Gold-Bug*, which likewise featured a quest for pirate booty. What's more interesting: the same real-life pirate shows up in both Irving's and Poe's stories. Which means there's a nugget of truth at the heart of the buried treasure story after all, and that truth-nugget was named Captain Kidd.

William Kidd was born in Scotland in 1645, and after a promising sailing career as a young man, he hustled his way to full-fledged "privateer"—a captain authorized to commandeer and raid foreign ships. There was a fine line between privateer and pirate, and unscrupulous privateers frequently drifted over to the more lucrative side of things. By 1695, Kidd had befriended Lord Bellomont, the governor of New York and Massachusetts, and the two worked out a profit-sharing agreement. Kidd and his crew would patrol the seas, protecting English vessels and harassing French-flagged ships, with Bellomont and his co-investors bankrolling the operation. They even outfitted Kidd with a fancy new ship! It must have looked promising on paper, but things didn't end well.

In 1698, Kidd's crew raided a ship named the *Quedagh Merchant*. The vessel was Armenian, but sailing with a French pass, so it technically was fair game—and it was a jackpot. The ship was so laden with gold, silver, and other valuables that Kidd and his crew would have been fabulously rich. Except…it turns out the captain of the *Quedagh Merchant* was English, and his cargo was property of the well-connected French East India Company.

When British authorities heard what had happened, they feared that Kidd—already on thin ice due to rumors of borderline behavior—had moved into outright piracy, and they decided to shut him down. Kidd found out that a warrant had been issued for his arrest, so he decided to make a low-profile trip to New England and arrange some help from his buddy Lord Bellomont.

In what surely seemed like a great idea at the time, Kidd buried some treasure on Gardiners Island (near Long Island), hoping to use it as a bargaining chip. Then he sailed on to Boston, where his friend was waiting—but it was a trap. The governor threw Kidd in jail and ultimately delivered him to England to stand trial. Adding insult to injury, Bellomont had Kidd's treasure dug up to be used as evidence against him. Not cool!

Kidd's trial was a spectacle, and the prosecution intended to make an example of him. Desperate, Kidd claimed that in exchange for leniency, he'd be happy to direct the authorities to even more buried treasure left behind in his old haunts. Unfortunately, they didn't bite. Kidd was convicted of piracy and murder—the last charge stemming from an incident in which he'd mortally wounded a crewman during an argument—and he was hanged in 1701. Following his execution, Kidd's body was locked in a gibbet (a form-fitting iron cage) and dangled over the River Thames for more than two years as a warning to anyone contemplating piracy. (Subtlety was not the point here.)

By now the legend of Captain Kidd—and the romanticization of buried treasure—had firmly taken root. Almost overnight, Kidd went from unlucky privateer to near-mythical pirate. Who could say what dazzling riches might still be out there, just waiting to be discovered? And yet, despite some tantalizing leads over the years, Captain Kidd's rumored buried treasure remains as elusive now as it was three centuries ago.

VEXING VEXILLOLOGY

BY COLIN

Oh, no! I assembled an awesome quiz on world flags, but nobody told me this book was in black and white. Luckily, each of the flags I chose has only two colors—white plus another color—and a design that doesn't match any other flag. So if you really know your vexillology (the study of flags, natch), this should be a breeze, right?

For each flag, you'll need to answer two questions: the name of the country/region it represents, and the color shown as black in the illustration. Things start out easy enough, but only the savviest travelers will get all 12 correct. So grab your black-and-white passport, and let's go!

This must be what it's like to be a vexillologist's dog.

CHRIS

QUESTIONS

1.

Flag of _____

White and _____

2.

Flag of _____

White and _____

3.

Flag of _____

White and _____

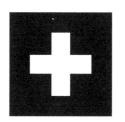

4.

Flag of _____

White and _____

5.

Flag of _____

White and _____

6.

Flag of _____

White and _____

7.

Flag of _____

White and _____

8.

Flag of _____

White and _____

9.

Flag of _____

White and _____

10.

Flag of _____

White and _____

11.

Flag of _____

White and _____

12.

Flag of _____

White and _____

1. Flag of **Canada** = white and **red**.

2. Flag of **Israel** = white and **blue**.

3. Flag of **Japan** = white and **red**.

4. Flag of **Switzerland** = white and **red**. Switzerland is one of only two countries with a square flag, Vatican City being the other.

5. Flag of **Greece** = white and **blue**.

6. Flag of **Saudi Arabia** = white and **green**. The calligraphic Arabic script on Saudi Arabia's flag translates to "There is no god but God; Muhammad is the Messenger of God."

7. Flag of **Hong Kong** = white and **red**. This highly autonomous Special Administrative Region of the People's Republic of China—formerly a British colony—flies its own flag along with the Chinese national flag.

8. Flag of **Scotland** = white and **blue**.

9. Flag of **Turkey** = white and **red**.

10. Flag of **Greenland** = white and **red**.

11. Flag of **Honduras** = white and **blue**.

12. Flag of **Qatar** = white and **maroon**. With an unusual aspect ratio of 28:11, Qatar's is the only national flag that's more than twice as wide as it is tall.

MONEY MAKES THE WORLD GO 'ROUND

BY COLIN

In 2002 the euro replaced the old currencies of 12 European nations. This was a big step forward for a unified Europe, but oh man, did we lose a lot of good currency trivia. In one fell swoop, we lost the German mark, the French franc, and the Greek drachma. (I mean, it's so much fun to say—*drachma*!) So to celebrate the good old days of currency variety, let's nerd out with a money-matching quiz.

On the top you've got a list of foreign currencies (common names), and on the bottom is a list of countries from around the world—you match 'em up! (There are no duplicate answers.)

CURRENCY NAMES

1. ____ Shekel
2. ____ Won
3. ____ Bolívar
4. ____ Rupee
5. ____ Ringgit

6. ____ Lira
7. ____ Rand
8. ____ Dinar
9. ____ Vatu
10. ____ Złoty

11. ____ Ruble
12. ____ Baht
13. ____ Rial
14. ____ Dollar
15. ____ Krone

COUNTRIES

A. Poland
B. Venezuela
C. Israel
D. Iraq
E. Malaysia

F. Russia
G. Denmark
H. South Africa
I. Turkey
J. India

K. South Korea
L. Thailand
M. Iran
N. Vanuatu
O. Jamaica

One Beaver Buck

ONE BEAVER BUCK

1 1

ONE
BEAVER BUCK

1 1

GOOD JOB, BRAIN!
GJB55378008 C

Sarah Bellum
Treasurer of Castoria

BEAVERSON

Joseph Triviani
Secretary of the Treasury

ANSWERS

1. **C.** Israel (Shekel)

2. **K.** South Korea (Won)

3. **B.** Venezuela (Bolívar—This national currency is named in honor of Simón Bolívar, the most prominent figure in the fight for Venezuelan independence nearly two centuries ago.)

4. **J.** India (Rupee)

5. **E.** Malaysia (Ringgit)

6. **I.** Turkey (Lira—As alluded to in the introduction, that killjoy euro got rid of the Italian lira in 2002. At least Turkey is still cool.)

7. **H.** South Africa (Rand)

8. **D.** Iraq (Dinar)

9. **N.** Vanuatu (Vatu—Please tell me you got this one; it's right there in the name!)

10. **A.** Poland (Złoty—The letter ł in Polish is pronounced almost like *w* in English.)

11. **F.** Russia (Ruble)

12. **L.** Thailand (Baht)

13. **M.** Iran (Rial)

14. **O.** Jamaica (Dollar)

15. **G.** Denmark (Krone—Like the Norwegian krone and the Swedish krona, the name means "crown.")

Oh, rupees! They use those in the Kingdom of Hyrule in *The Legend of Zelda*!

CHRIS

I'll give you half credit for that one, Chris.

COLIN

UM, ACTUALLY...

BY COLIN

If you spend enough time inhaling factoids and trawling wikis, you'll inevitably encounter the bane of all trivia-lovers: *bad facts*. The bad fact has numerous spawning grounds: workplace know-it-alls, half-baked trivia books, even the underside of fruity beverage lids (you know whom I'm talking about). Most of these scraps of misinformation are so silly they're hardly worth fighting over—I still don't know why people believe a duck's quack has no echo—but some are so faux-profound (fauxfound?) that they take on a life of their own, seeping into our collectively accepted knowledge.

One of my favorite recurring segments on *Good Job, Brain!* is "Um, Actually...," in which listeners take us to task for our (hopefully infrequent) factual flubs, and we get to set the trivia record straight. So in the spirit of "Um, Actually...," I invite you to help me stomp out some "classics" of false knowledge. I've chosen my five favorite (for lack of a better word) Bad Facts from the fields of science and history—I bet you've heard some if not all of these—and together we'll explore why, exactly, they're so wrong.

"THE GREAT WALL OF CHINA IS THE ONLY STRUCTURE VISIBLE FROM SPACE."

This one is so resilient I almost feel sorry for squashing it. Sometimes you'll hear that the Great Wall is the only structure visible from space, sometimes that it's the only structure visible from the moon. Both flavors of this bad fact are demonstrably false.

Also visible from space: your butt. OH SNAP.

CHRIS

Let's start by busting the first version of the claim. For that I'll simply share the words of Alan Bean, the fourth person to walk on the moon: "The only thing you can see from the moon is a beautiful sphere, mostly white (clouds), some blue (ocean), patches of yellow (deserts), and every once in a while some green vegetation. No man-made object is visible on this scale. In fact, when first leaving Earth's orbit and only a few thousand miles away, no man-made object is visible at that point either."[16]

---

16. Tom Burnam, *More Misinformation* (New York: Ballantine Books, 1981),100.

So that rules out any romantic wall-gazing from the moon. "Okay, but what about lower orbits?" you helpfully ask, in mock disbelief. Sure, if you're in what's called a *low Earth orbit* (the region where the International Space Station circles the Earth, at a tiny fraction of the distance to the moon), you can *maybe* see the Great Wall, if conditions are *just right*. But once you're close enough to catch a glimpse of the Great Wall, you can also easily make out other signs of humanity, like freeways, canals, stadiums, and airports.

I'll let another professional space-goer have the last word on this one. Astronaut Chris Hadfield said of the Great Wall, "It'd be hard to see from an airplane in a lot of places. Even from the Space Station, which is only 400 kilometers up, we can't see it—it's like they were trying to hide it from astronauts."[17]

"CHRISTOPHER COLUMBUS HAD TROUBLE FINDING SUPPORT FOR HIS VOYAGE BECAUSE PEOPLE THOUGHT THE EARTH WAS FLAT."

It's true that Christopher Columbus initially failed to persuade several kings and queens to finance his exploration of a western route to the Indies (Asia). And there certainly were people in 1492 who believed the Earth was flat—heck, there are people *today* who still believe it—but even in Columbus's time, every scientist and sailor of note would have agreed the Earth is round. Competent royal advisors knew this as well, so it wasn't fear of tumbling over the edge of the globe that kept Europe's royal purses closed.

No, the primary reason Columbus was turned down so many times was that prospective backers didn't trust his wildly optimistic estimate of the distance west to Asia. And sure enough, he was way off! Columbus calculated his route based on faulty data, and in reality he would have been thousands of miles short. A journey that long was beyond the limits of any ship at the time—the fleet just wouldn't be able to carry sufficient provisions. If Columbus hadn't fortuitously bumped into the "New World" en route, there's no telling what fate he would have met.

So how did this bad fact become so entrenched? Washington Irving's widely read biography of Columbus from 1828 appears to have played a large part. In the book, Irving implies that belief in a flat Earth was common, especially among the powers that be in the Catholic

---

17. Chris Hadfield, interview by Bob McDonald, *Quirks and Quarks*, CBC/Radio-Canada, published November 20, 2010, accessed April 5, 2016, www.cbc.ca/video/news/audioplayer.html?clipid=1653290421.

Church. Unfortunately for proud defenders of trivia and circumnavigation, this false view of 15th-century science wormed its way into many history books.

"THE GREAT SPHINX'S NOSE WAS BLOWN OFF."

Yes, the Great Sphinx of Giza is missing its nose. No, it had nothing to do with cannons, tanks, artillery, bullets, gunpowder, or explosives of any kind.

The most frequently repeated version of this bad fact pins the blame for blasting the Sphinx's nose on Napoleon's army at the turn of the 19th century. Another version names Turks as the culprits. Even British troops have been blamed, as yet another variant of the story accuses them of destroying the nose in a particularly mean-spirited round of target practice during World War I.

I'm here to let Napoleon (not to mention the Turks and Brits) off the hook. Photographs from the 1800s prove the Sphinx's nose was already long gone by then, and there are earlier sketches—indeed, from before Napoleon was even born—depicting the same thing.

So…what happened to the nose? Reliable historical accounts say it was destroyed in 1378 by a local religious leader and iconoclast. Angered by citizens honoring the Sphinx, he ordered the defacement of the monumental statue. (He apparently paid for the act of vandalism with his life—enraged worshippers reportedly had him lynched.)

"GLASS MAY LOOK SOLID, BUT IT IS AN EXTREMELY SLOW-MOVING LIQUID."

I read this "fact" in a trivia collection when I was 10 or 11 years old, and I got a good 20 years of use out of it before I discovered I'd been lied to—and had unintentionally lied to others! So let me (ahem) be perfectly clear: no, glass is not a slow-moving liquid.

"Ah, but centuries-old window panes are thicker on the bottom," you might hear from doubters. While this is true, it's not evidence of glass "flowing" downward over the years. Panes being thicker on one side is merely an artifact of older glass-making techniques; and if you were a glazier installing windows in those days, it naturally made sense to set the thicker edge of a pane on the bottom of the frame.

To be fair, glass is unusual in that it's an *amorphous solid*, meaning its molecules don't have the highly ordered arrangements we find in most other solids. Regardless, once molten glass cools, it truly does behave like a "traditional" solid. So go ahead and build your dream glass house, my friend; it won't slowly melt around you. (But watch it with the stones, will you?)

"WATER NATURALLY SWIRLS CLOCKWISE OR COUNTERCLOCKWISE AS IT GOES DOWN A DRAIN, DEPENDING ON WHETHER YOU'RE IN THE NORTHERN OR SOUTHERN HEMISPHERE."

I guarantee one thing: however long ago you first heard this one, someone had you beat by at least 50 years. And it was just as wrong then as it is now.

The science supposedly underlying this easily tested claim is the "Coriolis force," which affects motion relative to a rotating frame of reference (in this case, our lovely rotating planet). The Coriolis force is real, but with regard to the Earth's rotation it only comes into play with large-scale phenomena like weather patterns and ocean currents (which do indeed tend to rotate in opposite directions above and below the Equator).

Though it's always cool to be reminded we're sitting on a giant sphere spinning in space, the comparatively minuscule amount of water in your sink or bathtub (or even your swimming pool) is too small to be affected by the Earth's rotation. Which means your rubber duckie is just as likely to swirl in either direction while riding out that cute little whirlpool celebrating the end of your bath.

JAPAN OR NOT JAPAN?

BY CHRIS

After Dana's "Belgium or Not Belgium?" quiz, which so helpfully divided the world into two distinct (if highly irregular) portions, I wanted to do a similar quiz for the country in which I lived for two years: Japan!

Some of the statements below describe Japan, and some describe not-Japan. Circle the letters of the statements that describe Japan. When you're done, you can rearrange the circled letters into something you may want to avoid (or try!) if you travel to Japan.

STATEMENTS

Are these things true about Japan or Not Japan?

A. Acupuncture was invented here, sometime prior to 100 BC.

B. What's generally considered to be the world's first novel was written here.

F. The world's most expensive watermelon (in 2008) was purchased here.

H. The world's most expensive fish (in 2013) was purchased here.

I. Raw horse meat is often served here, euphemistically called "cherry blossom meat" (after its pinkish tinge).

L. More than 85 percent of the coffee grown in Jamaica is sent to this country.

M. The urban legend of "fan death"—the idea that sleeping with a fan blowing on you will kill you—is prevalent here.

N. Ramen was invented here sometime before 1900.

O. This country has the longest average life expectancy in the world.

P. Fireworks were invented here in the 7th century.

Q. This country is located on a peninsula.

S. Nintendo was founded here in 1889.

W. Ronald McDonald is known here as "Donald McDonald."

A. **Not Japan**. Acupuncture was invented in China.

B. **Japan**. *The Tale of Genji*, written in the 11th century by Lady Murasaki Shikibu.

F. **Japan**. A black Hokkaido Densuke watermelon sold for more than $6,800.

H. **Japan**. In January 2013, a bluefin tuna sold for a whopping $1.8 million.

I. **Japan**. Be careful if anyone asks you to eat "cherry blossom" sashimi.

L. **Japan**. They love their Jamaican coffee, I guess.

M. **Not Japan**. It's Korea that's frightened of "fan death."

N. **Not Japan**. Ramen originally came to Japan as "Chinese soba."

O. **Japan**. Average life expectancy is 84, the highest in the world.

P. **Not Japan**. Fireworks came from China.

Q. **Not Japan**. Japan is an archipelago, a small group of islands.

S. **Japan**. Nintendo was originally a maker of *hanafuda*, Japanese playing cards.

W. **Japan**. There's also a statue of Colonel Sanders outside many of the Kentucky Fried Chicken restaurants in Japan.

Rearrange the letters of the "Japan" entries and you get BLOWFISH, a sometimes-poisonous delicacy that you might want to eat (or avoid) on a trip to Japan.

BRAD PITT OR LASERS? PART III

BY COLIN

Okay, smartypants, you've conquered the first two installments of "Brad Pitt or Lasers?" and are feeling pretty cocky. So this final entry in the series, with the thinnest margins yet, will push your date-estimating skills to the limit. As always, your job is to say which is older.

(For a person, this means the year he or she was born; for a landmark, it means the year construction was completed; for a movie, TV show, or product, it means the year it was released.)

QUESTIONS

1. Which is older: **Hugh Hefner** or **sliced bread**?

2. Which is older: **Google** or *The Matrix*?

3. Which is older: **The Rolling Stones** or **AstroTurf**?

4. Which is older: **Disneyland** or **Madonna**?

5. Which is older: *Star Trek* or the **Super Bowl**?

6. Which is older: **LSD** or **SPAM**?

7. Which is older: **gummy bears** or **Band-Aids**?

8. Which is older: *Sesame Street* or the **moon landing**?

1. **Hugh Hefner** is older than sliced bread. *Playboy* magazine founder Hugh Hefner was born in 1926; the first automatic bread-slicing machine designed for commercial use was patented by Otto Rohwedder in 1928.

2. **Google** is older than *The Matrix*. Internet and technology giant Google was founded in 1998; cinematic blockbuster *The Matrix* was released in 1999.

3. **The Rolling Stones** are older than AstroTurf. The venerable rock band was formed in 1962; the Monsanto Company patented AstroTurf-brand artificial turf in 1964. (Originally marketed as ChemGrass, it was renamed after being installed in Houston's Astrodome.)

4. **Disneyland** is older than Madonna. Walt Disney's world-famous amusement park opened its doors in 1955; singer and pop icon Madonna was born in 1958.

5. **Star Trek** is older than the Super Bowl. Producer Gene Roddenberry's landmark TV show *Star Trek* premiered on NBC in 1966; the first Super Bowl was played in 1967, matching up the AFL's Kansas City Chiefs and the NFL's Green Bay Packers (the Packers won, 35–10).

6. **SPAM** is older than LSD. Hormel Foods introduced its SPAM canned meat in 1937; Swiss chemist Albert Hoffman synthesized LSD (lysergic acid diethylamide) in 1938 while working for Sandoz Pharmaceuticals.

7. **Band-Aids** are older than gummy bears. Band-Aid adhesive bandages were introduced in 1920 by the Johnson & Johnson Company; gummy bears were invented in 1922 by confectioner Hans Riegel, Sr., of Bonn, Germany, and sold through his company Haribo (an abbreviation of Hans Riegel, Bonn).

8. The **moon landing** is older than Sesame Street. Astronaut Neil Armstrong set foot on the moon on July 20, 1969, as part of NASA's historic Apollo 11 mission; beloved children's TV show *Sesame Street* debuted on November 10, 1969. (So close!)

ANGELS AND DEVILS

BY COLIN

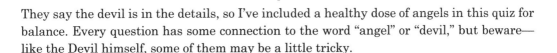

They say the devil is in the details, so I've included a healthy dose of angels in this quiz for balance. Every question has some connection to the word "angel" or "devil," but beware—like the Devil himself, some of them may be a little tricky.

QUESTIONS

1. What major city was originally named El Pueblo de Nuestra Señora la Reina de los Ángeles del Río de Porciúncula?

2. Pound for pound, what animal has the strongest bite of any living creature?

3. In the whiskey- and wine-making industries, what is "the Angel's Share"?

4. In the Catholic Church, what was the common name for someone who held the title "Promoter of the Faith"?

5. What record-holding natural landmark was unknown to the outside world until it was spotted by American pilot Jimmie Angel in 1933?

6. What modern retelling of the Faust legend was a smash hit on Broadway, running for more than 1,000 performances beginning in 1955?

7. What striking rock formation was prominently featured in director Steven Spielberg's classic sci-fi film *Close Encounters of the Third Kind*?

8. The name of what common bread can be translated into English as "Devil fart"?

1. **Los Angeles**. In English the original name of the city translates to "The Town of Our Lady the Queen of Angels of the Porciúncula River." (The Porciúncula River is what the Los Angeles River was called at the time.)

2. **The Tasmanian Devil**. Using a measure called the "bite force quotient," or BFQ—essentially the ratio of bite strength to body size—this feisty marsupial scores an impressive 181. That puts it well ahead of other fearsome biters such as tigers (with a BFQ of 127) and gray wolves (BFQ 136).

3. **The portion lost to evaporation**. Wine and whiskey aged in wooden barrels loses a small amount of volume over time due to water and/or alcohol evaporation. A small price to pay to keep the angels happy!

4. **The Devil's Advocate**. Historically, the Promoter of the Faith (or Devil's Advocate) was a lawyer appointed to play the role of skeptic during canonization proceedings. On the opposing side was the Promoter of the Cause (or God's Advocate). Eventually, "Devil's Advocate" came to mean anyone who adopts a skeptical or contrary position for the sake of argument. (This role in the canonization process was more or less eliminated in the 1980s.)

5. **Angel Falls**. Topping out at just over 3,200 feet, this Venezuelan waterfall is the highest in the world. Jimmie Angel discovered the falls while scouting from the air for deposits of precious metals. It was named in Angel's honor, and his ashes were sprinkled over the falls in 1960.

6. **Damn Yankees**. Based on *The Year the Yankees Lost the Pennant*, Douglass Wallop's novel about a baseball fan who makes a deal with the Devil, *Damn Yankees* was also made into a hit movie in 1958. (Coincidentally, the Yankees won the World Series that year.)

7. **Devils Tower**. This Wyoming landmark was the first United States National Monument, dedicated by President Theodore Roosevelt in 1906. (And yes, there's no apostrophe in the official name.)

8. **Pumpernickel**. "Pumper" comes from an old German word meaning "fart," and "nickel" in this case is a form of the name Nicholas, often associated with devils, goblins, and demons. "Devil fart" (or perhaps "goblin fart") may have been a reference to the, uh, digestive issues one might experience when eating this heavy, coarse bread.

> Who doesn't want devil fart bread?
>
> **DANA**

COMMON THREAD

BY COLIN

They say three is a magic number, so I'm giving you a group of three people, places, or things for each question in this quiz. Here's the twist: you have to tell me the common thread that unites all three. (And "I've never heard of any of them" doesn't count, smartypants.)

QUESTIONS

1. What do these places have in common?

    - Singapore

    - Monaco

    - Vatican City

2. What do these animals have in common?

    - Polar bear

    - Giraffe

    - Chow chow

3. What do these famous writers have in common?

    - George Eliot

    - Isak Dinesen

    - George Sand

4. What do these countries have in common (aside from the obvious)?

    - Luxembourg

    - Laos

    - Lesotho

5. What do these edible plants have in common?

   - Potatoes
   - Tomatoes
   - Rhubarb

6. What do these well-known books have in common?

   - *The Trial*, by Franz Kafka
   - *A Moveable Feast*, by Ernest Hemingway
   - *The Master and Margarita*, by Mikhail Bulgakov

7. What do these Academy Award–winning actors have in common?

   - Tom Hanks
   - Katharine Hepburn
   - Spencer Tracy

8. What do these words have in common?

   - Avatar
   - Mantra
   - Pundit

1. **They are all city-states**. In fact, they're generally regarded as the only true city-states today, though other highly autonomous regions and micro-nations are sometimes informally grouped with them.

2. **They all have blue or blue-black tongues**. (The polar bear's tongue color can vary the most of these three animals, from a light blue tinge to almost black.)

3. **They are all women who wrote their best-known works under male pseudonyms**. Isak Dinesen, author of *Out of Africa*, was a pen name of Karen Blixen (1885–1962). George Eliot, author of *Middlemarch* and *Silas Marner*, was the pseudonym of Mary Ann Evans (1819–1880). Amantine-Lucile-Aurore Dupin (1804–1876) wrote prolifically under the name George Sand, including the novels *Indiana* and *Valentine*.

4. **They are all landlocked countries**. Not only that, but Lesotho is one of only three nations to be completely surrounded by a single country (South Africa). The other two are San Marino and Vatican City, both surrounded by Italy.

5. **They all have poisonous leaves**. Potatoes and tomatoes are members of the nightshade family (*Solanaceae*), and their leaves contain varying levels of toxic solanine. Rhubarb isn't a nightshade, but its leaves are high in poisonous oxalic acid, among other potentially toxic substances.

6. **They were all published posthumously**. *The Trial* and *A Moveable Feast* both appeared within a few years of Kafka's and Hemingway's deaths, respectively, compiled by friends or family. But in the case of *Master and Margarita*, it took more than 25 years after Bulgakov's death for his masterpiece to be released.

7. **They all won Oscars in consecutive years**. Hanks won the Best Actor award for *Philadelphia* (1993) and *Forrest Gump* (1994); Hepburn was named Best Actress for *Guess Who's Coming to Dinner* (1967) and *The Lion in Winter* (1968,

in a rare Oscars tie with Barbra Streisand for her role in *Funny Girl*); and Tracy won Best Actor Oscars for *Captains Courageous* (1937) and *Boys Town* (1938).

8. **They are all borrowed from Sanskrit**. "Avatar" derives from *avatāra*, meaning "descent" (in the sense of a deity descending to Earth in a physical form). "Pundit" comes to us from *pandita*, which means "learned man" (a charitable label for many of today's TV news pundits). And "mantra" is the same word in Sanskrit, where it means, essentially, "the thought behind a ritualized action."

STUFF
YO' FACE

THE CAST OF *GOOD JOB, BRAIN!* IS PROUD
TO SAY THAT WE EAT FOOD OFTEN.

**HERE ARE OUR FAVORITE FACTS FIGURES
ABOUT DELICIOUS COMESTIBLES.**

THE OTHER TOROIDAL BREAKFAST

BY CHRIS

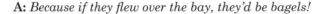

Q: *Why do seagulls fly over the sea?*

A: *Because if they flew over the bay, they'd be bagels!*

That classic joke always gets me thinking about my favorite breakfast food: carbs. And then, my favorite type of carb: bagels. When I lived in Japan, bagels were the only American food I desperately tried to find a decent version of but couldn't. If a coffee shop had bagels, they had no toaster; if they had a toaster, they had no schmear. It was a tough time, bagelwise.

So one day I decided to go looking for information about the history of this hole-y grail of all morning foods, and this was the first thing I found in *Wikipedia*'s "History" section:

> *Contrary to some beliefs, the bagel was not created in the shape of a stirrup to commemorate the victory of Poland's King John III Sobieski over the Ottoman Empire at the Battle of Vienna in 1683.*

I know what you're thinking: "What? But I'd always heard that the bagel was created in the shape of a stirrup to commemorate the victory of Poland's King John III Sobieski over the Ottoman Empire at the Battle of Vienna in 1683!" Well, consider that myth *busted*.

So, why the hole? Probably for the same reason that donuts have holes: so they cook more evenly, and you're not left with a doughy or raw center to worry about.

Bagels were invented in Poland sometime prior to the 16th century. Poland's Jewish community had loved bagels for centuries, bringing them to New York when they emigrated to America. At the time, most bagels being made in New York (and thus America) were from bakeries that belonged to the Bagel Bakers Local 338 union.[18] The group guarded its secrets, and its memberships, closely. At one point, membership spots were only given out to the sons of current members, and meetings were conducted only in Yiddish.

---

18. "The Story of the New York Bagel Union," New Yorker Bagels, published April 15, 2014, accessed July 14, 2016, http://newyorkerbagels.com/the-story-of-the-new-york-bagel-union.

GOOD JOB, **BRAIN!**

How did bagels go from localized ethnic food to something you can buy in Starbucks around the world? Much of the credit is given to Harry Lender. Born in Poland at the turn of the 20th century, Lender moved his family to New Jersey in response to the increasing anti-Semitism in his homeland. He began working at a bagel bakery, saved his money, and eventually bought a bakery of his own in New Haven, Connecticut. At that time, bagels were such a localized food product that New Haven was a largely untapped market.

Lender's bagels became so popular that in the 1960s his company started experimenting with freezing them. This was a solution to a particular problem of the bagel seller. By and large, they'd sell thousands of bagels on Saturday night and Sunday morning, for the day's big breakfast. But during the rest of the week, demand was low. So they perfected a method of baking bagels throughout the week, freezing them, and then selling them on Sunday.

Well, at that point they could start selling frozen bagels to hotels, resorts, and other such clients—and soon after that, directly to supermarkets, bagged up in the freezer section. Now bagels could be shipped easily, and what was an odd local ethnic food became commonplace all over the country.

The rise in popularity wasn't without its dissidents. "Bagels Are Now Fast Food, and Purists Do a Slow Boil," read a *New York Times* headline from 1993. The story noted that even in 1974, some shops advertising bagels faced a quizzical public who thought they were selling beagles for breakfast.[19]

I'll leave you with some chewy trivia: bagels have grown quite a bit larger over the years. When Harry Lender started making bagels, they would have been small, three-ounce portions. Today's bagels have ballooned to more than twice their original size.[20] (As has your author. Thanks, bagels!)

19. Molly O'Neill, "Bagels Are Now a Fast Food, and Purists Do a Slow Boil," *New York Times*, April 25, 1993, www.nytimes.com/1993/04/25/us/bagels-are-now-a-fast-food-and-purists-do-a-slow-boil.html.

20. E. D. Levine, "Was Life Better When Bagels Were Smaller?" *New York Times*, December 31, 2003, www.nytimes.com/2003/12/31/dining/was-life-better-when-bagels-were-smaller.html

COCKTAIL!

BY DANA

In addition to usually being delicious, cocktails are a fun source of trivia nuggets. From antimalarial treatments to 15th-century Venetian artists, can you match up these cocktails with trivia about them?

COCKTAILS

A. Appletini

B. Bellini

C. Bloody Mary

D. Cosmopolitan

E. Daiquiri

F. Gin and Tonic

G. Hurricane

H. Mai Tai

I. Mimosa

J. Mint Julep

K. Old Fashioned

L. Piña Colada

M. Tequila Sunrise

N. White Russian

CLUES

1. _____ The first documented definition of "cocktail" describes ingredients in this drink.

2. _____ A district in Cuba gives this drink its name.

3. _____ This drink gets its name from a Tahitian word meaning "good."

4. _____ After being featured in a 1970s song by Rupert Holmes, this drink gained worldwide renown.

5. _____ This drink gets its name from a type of lamp.

6. _____ Its combination of sweet, salty, sour, and savory flavors are why this drink is considered the world's most complexly flavored cocktail.

7. _____ Though this drink was invented in the Midwest in the 1970s, it's strongly associated with New York City and a late '90s/early 2000s TV show.

8. _____ Churchill Downs and the Kentucky Derby have promoted this drink since 1938.

9. _____ This drink was probably named for a flower that shares the same color.

10. _____ This drink got its name because it contains vodka, not because of its country of origin.

11. _____ A 15th-century Venetian artist gives this drink its name.

12. _____ Both an Eagles song and a Mel Gibson movie share this drink's name.

13. _____ The army of the British East India Company introduced this drink in the early 19th century.

14. _____ In 2010, Facebook head Mark Zuckerberg called this the official drink of his company.

1. **K. Old Fashioned**. In 1806, *The Balance and Columbian Repository* (Hudson, NY) defined a "cocktail" as "a stimulating liquor, composed of spirits of any kind, sugar, water, and bitters" all the ingredients in a traditional Old Fashioned.

2. **E. Daiquiri**. The village of Daiquirí, Cuba, is about 14 miles east of Santiago de Cuba and is home to an iron mine. Legend has it that the cocktail was invented by American mining engineers working in Cuba, who named the drink after the area.

3. **H. Mai Tai**. The Mai Tai was invented by Victor J. Bergeron at his restaurant Trader Vic's in Oakland, CA. The story goes that after tasting the drink, one of his Tahitian friends said, "Maita'i roa ae," which means "very good" in Tahitian.

4. **L. Piña Colada**. The name of the drink is prominently featured in Rupert Holmes' 1979 earworm "Escape (The Piña Colada Song)"—*If you like Piña Coladas and getting caught in the rain…*

5. **G. Hurricane**. In the mid-1940s in New Orleans, there was a shortage of bourbon and Scotch but a surplus of rum, an unpopular alcohol at the time. In order to clear out his rum inventory, a New Orleans bar owner mixed a fruity rum drink in hurricane lamp–shaped glasses and sold it to sailors. The drinks were a huge hit.

6. **C. Bloody Mary**. According to Neil C. Da Costa, an expert in the chemical analysis of flavors, "The Bloody Mary has been called the world's most complex cocktail, and from the standpoint of flavor chemistry, you've got a blend of hundreds of flavor compounds that act on the taste senses. It covers almost the entire range of human taste sensations—sweet, salty, sour and umami or savory—but not bitter."[21]

---

21. Michael Bernstein and Michael Woods, "Creating the Perfect Bloody Mary: Good Chemistry of Fresh Ingredients," American Chemical Society, published March 29, 2011, accessed July 20, 2016, www.acs.org/content/acs/en/press-room/newsreleases/2011/march/creating-the-perfect-bloody-mary-good-chemistry-of-fresh-ingredients.html.

7. **D. Cosmopolitan**. The TV show *Sex and the City* is credited with a surge in popularity of the Cosmopolitan. Sarah Jessica Parker's character Carrie Bradshaw regularly drank the cocktail. Reference is made to its popularity in the film adaptation when Miranda asks, "Why did we ever stop drinking these?" And Carrie responds, "Because everyone else started."

8. **J. Mint Julep**. The mint julep is the traditional beverage of the Kentucky Oaks and Kentucky Derby horse races. Though different alcohols have served as the base for this cocktail over time, it's become commonly accepted that a mint julep must be made with Kentucky bourbon whiskey.

I once won us a point at a pub quiz for guessing the name of the cocktail featured on *Sex and the City*. It was a Flirtini and no, I am not proud of myself.

CHRIS

9. **I. Mimosa**. The mimosa tree or *Acacia dealbata* is known for its bright yellow flowers.

10. **N. White Russian**. The "Russian" in the name is a reference to the vodka in the cocktail, while "white" refers to the cream. The progenitor of the White Russian cocktail, the Black Russian, was invented in Belgium.

11. **B. Bellini**. The inventor of the Bellini said the drink's peachy color reminded him of the toga worn by a saint in a painting by 15th-century Venetian artist Giovanni Bellini.

12. **M. Tequila Sunrise**. The Eagles' 1973 song and the 1988 film starring Mel Gibson both share the name of the drink invented in 1970.

13. **F. Gin and Tonic**. In the 19th century, British officers in tropical areas mixed gin with the quinine tonics they took for preventing and treating malaria to make them more palatable.

14. **A. Appletini**. In the film *The Social Network* (2010), Sean Parker introduces Mark Zuckerberg to Appletinis. After seeing the film, Zuckerberg denied ever having had an Appletini but said he'd make it the official drink of Facebook.

FRAUDULENT FOODS AND FLAVOR FOOLERS

BY KAREN

I have an appreciation for and deep obsession with impostor foods. I'm not sitting here eating imitation crab and thinking I'm dining on Alaskan king crab legs, or equating Cheez Whiz with the best Cheddar from the English countryside. However, there are some foods out there that aren't quit so blatant when masquerading as the real deal.

WASABI

Wa-say-it-ain't-so! Only a teensy fraction of the human population has ever tasted real wasabi, and for good reason. The wasabi plant (also known as Japanese horseradish) is quite tricky to cultivate, which leads to a hefty price tag for such a weird-looking lump. And even if chefs get their hands on the real thing, wasabi is super high-maintenance and needs to be freshly grated right before serving, because the heat and flavor dissipate in minutes. So that bright green paste we're used to seeing in restaurants and food stores is usually made of western horseradish (which is white), green coloring, mustard, and other additives. The result is something that's a lot cheaper and available than real wasabi, producing the same burn-up-your-nose-tubes effect even though it's a fake.

SUPERMARKET BLUEBERRY MUFFINS

Well, actually, it doesn't stop with muffins: bagels, cookies, cereals, oatmeal, and bars—many food items you find in supermarkets that evoke the homey baked blueberry feel aren't made of fresh or even dried blueberries. Those dark purple bits you see in mini one-bite blueberry muffins are mostly clumps of dyed sugar or dried apples with blueberry flavoring added. But c'mon, honestly: this shouldn't be that surprising, since baking with real blueberries often leads to messy tie-dye explosions in your muffins.

PISTACHIO GELATO

Gelato aficionados will tell you that in order to gauge the quality of a gelato place, the telltale flavor to try is pistachio. It's one of the most counterfeited flavors. Naturally it comes down to moola once again. Besides the fact that pistachios are annoying to pry open, they aren't cheap. Pistachio ice creams can be faked just by using artificial flavoring, but the more common practice is to use almonds for most of the nuts, supplemented with some pistachios (and extra green coloring).

TRUFFLE OIL

Hold onto your hats, folks: commercial truffle oil does not contain any truffle. ANY truffle. Not even bits. I thought for years that truffle oil involved some laborious process of imbuing it with the essence of truffles pried from the jaws of trained search pigs oinking away in the countryside of France. No. Truffle oil is oil, all right, but what makes it fragrant is nothing but synthetic foolery. Commercial truffle oil uses the compound 2,4-dithiapentane to imitate that Earthy flavor. Though 2,4-dithiapentane can be found in real truffles, it is only one of *many, many, many* smelly compounds that make the real deal so complex and unique.

Heck, I guess I can stop squeezing this truffle now.

CHRIS

BUTTER POPCORN TOPPING

You might have seen the movie concession guy behind the counter pumping that bright yellow liquid all over your popcorn. It smells like butter, it tastes like butter, it looks like butter, but it's really just colored hydrogenated vegetable oil with butter flavoring. These flavored oils are much easier and cheaper to produce and can be stored much more easily than actual fresh butter. Come to think of it, when was the last time you had popcorn flavored with real butter? Probably not that often: a good chunk of butter (around 15 percent) is moisture, and that will break down the structural integrity of the popcorn. Try pouring real melted butter onto your popcorn, and you'll end up with something that tastes way better than the fake stuff but looks like wet papier mâché.

YOUR MEDICINE IS LIKE BAD LOVE

BY CHRIS

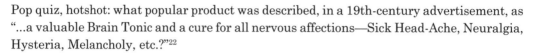

Pop quiz, hotshot: what popular product was described, in a 19th-century advertisement, as "...a valuable Brain Tonic and a cure for all nervous affections—Sick Head-Ache, Neuralgia, Hysteria, Melancholy, etc.?"[22]

That's right—it's good old Coca-Cola, which purported to derive its "medicinal" benefits from the coca plant (from whence also comes cocaine) and the kola nut. These days, we know that the only ailment Coca-Cola cures is Dry Cheeseburger Syndrome. But it certainly wasn't the only bogus medicine that's been peddled over the years. Here are three more crazy doses of snake oil.

CALOMEL

I'll say this for snake oil: at least it's harmless. A century ago, if you skipped the medicine show and went to an actual doctor, you were liable to be given a dose of actual poison. One of the most popular medications in pre–Civil War America was calomel. What is it? Mercurous chloride. Yep: patients were chugging mercury.

Calomel was widely used in the late 18th century to counteract yellow fever. You'd start vomiting pretty quickly due to all that poison you were drinking, and this was considered great because you were purging out all of the impurities. But no, now you had yellow fever *and* mercury poisoning. *Little Women* author Louisa May Alcott was given calomel and suffered from the effects of mercury poisoning for the rest of her life.

KICKAPOO INDIAN SAGWA

The premier product of the Kickapoo Indian Medicine Company (which had no connection whatsoever to the real-life Kickapoo tribe), this was sold at traveling medicine shows. It promised to cure whatever ailed you, and it was endorsed—in one of the earliest celebrity endorsements—by Wild West showman Buffalo Bill Cody. It was pretty much nothing.

---

22. John Burnett, *Liquid Pleasures: A Social History of Drinks in Modern Britain* (London: Routledge, 1999), 103.

GOOD JOB, **BRAIN!**

Another fine product of the Kickapoo Company was Kickapoo Indian Worm Killer. Read one 1903 newspaper advertisement: "If your child is restless at night, grinds its teeth, wets the bed, is constipated, craves indigestible food or is fretful and peevish, you can be sure it has Worms."[23] So basically, if your child acts like a child. But don't worry, parents, all your kids have to do is take Worm Killer pills and they'll expel all of those worms that are causing them to be peevish. Or rather, they'll poop out a bunch of little pieces of string, which had been carefully concealed in the pill.

HADACOL

Let's go back to happy, mostly harmless snake oil, shall we? The first half of the 20th century saw what is generally considered to be the last of the big traveling medicine shows—for a product called Hadacol. This was the brainchild of a U.S. Senator with the wonderful twisty-moustache name of Dudley J. LeBlanc, who toured the South in the Hadacol Goodwill Caravan.

Thousands of people came to see the biggest celebrities of the day perform—Judy Garland, Milton Berle, Bob Hope, Lucille Ball, everybody. There were songs: "Hadacol Boogie," for one, or "Everybody Loves That Hadacol." There was even a comic book, *Captain Hadacol*, in which our caped hero consumes tons of Hadacol and urges parents to give it to their kids.

So, what's in it? Well, apparently there actually were B vitamins in there, which *are* good for you. But the reason Hadacol was so great was that it was 12 percent alcohol. In other words, Captain Hadacol's superpower was being drunk in the daytime. "Dry counties," where straightforward alcoholic drinks couldn't be sold, loved it! Not to mention the kids.

But my favorite part of Hadacol is the name. In actuality, it's an abbreviation of the Happy Day Company, with an L added for LeBlanc. But if you asked its inventor *cum* moonshiner where he came up with the name, he'd have told you, "Well…I hadda call it *somethin'*."

---

23. "Your Child's Health," *Deseret News* (Salt Lake City, UT), April 15, 1903, https://news.google.com/newspapers?nid=Aul-kAQHnToC&dat=19030415&printsec=frontpage&hl=en.

DINER LINGO

BY CHRIS

Diners were the quintessential mid-20th-century American eatery, with grouchy waitresses named "Madge" and "Flo" serving greasy eggs and questionable gravy to travelers all over the United States. And with diners came diner lingo, a colorful jargon in which ordinary menu items became fanciful, often self-deprecating, sometimes kind-of-gross jokes.

If you walked into a diner and ordered "franks and beans," the waitress might shout back to the short-order cook, "Two bloodhounds on an island!" Ask for poached eggs on toast and you might hear, "Get this guy Adam and Eve on a raft!"

"Diner lingo was never intended for use in speeding up the order-to-table process," wrote Garrison Leykam in the book *Classic Diners of Connecticut*. "Rather, it was a spontaneously developed mnemonic means of making orders easier to hear and remember above the conversational din of the busy diner. It also provided patrons and employees with a free form of entertainment."

Some diner lingo actually entered common vernacular—it's believed that "over easy" and "sunny side up" were originally diner slang. Think you can work backward and figure out what classic diner dishes these bits of diner lingo are referring to?

SLANG

1. ____ "Jack Benny!"
2. ____ "Breath!"
3. ____ "Sweep the kitchen!"
4. ____ "Whistleberries!"
5. ____ "Burn one, and drag it through the garden!"
6. ____ "Atlanta special!"
7. ____ "Dog soup!"
8. ____ "First lady!"
9. ____ "Burn the British!"
10. ____ "Dry stack!"
11. ____ "Hot blonde with sand!"
12. ____ "Squeeze one!"

DISHES

A. Hash
B. Water
C. Coffee with cream and sugar
D. Garlic
E. Ribs
F. Orange juice
G. Coca-Cola
H. Toasted English muffin
I. Grilled American cheese sandwich with bacon
J. Beans
K. Pancakes, no butter or syrup
L. Well-done burger with lettuce, tomato, and onion

ANSWERS

✄

1. **I.** Grilled American cheese sandwich with bacon ("Jack Benny"—"GAC," pronounced "Jack," is a Grilled American Cheese, and a "Jack Benny" is a GAC with bacon.)

2. **D.** Garlic ("Breath")

3. **A.** Hash ("Sweep the kitchen"—Also known as "the gentleman will take a chance.")

4. **J.** Beans ("Whistleberries")

5. **L.** Well-done burger with lettuce, tomato, and onion ("Burn one, and drag it through the garden.")

6. **G.** Coca-Cola ("Atlanta special"—Also known as the "holy water of the South.")

7. **B.** Water ("Dog soup"—Also known as "Adam's ale" or "city juice.")

8. **E.** Ribs (First lady—Eve, the "first lady," was said to have been made from Adam's rib.)

9. **H.** Toasted English Muffin ("Burn the British")

10. **K.** Pancakes, no butter or syrup ("Dry stack")

11. **C.** Coffee with cream and sugar ("Hot blonde with sand")

12. **F.** Orange juice ("Squeeze one")

WOULD YOU CARE FOR A BOWL OF WORMS?

BY DANA

Mmm…worms. My favorite! Well, I guess they're only my favorite if they're made of pasta. Below are the names of some types of pasta and their literal translations from Italian to English. How many you can match up correctly?

ITALIAN PASTA NAMES

1. ____ Barbina
2. ____ Capellini
3. ____ Conchiglie
4. ____ Farfalle
5. ____ Fedelini
6. ____ Fettuccine
7. ____ Lasagna
8. ____ Linguine
9. ____ Orecchiette
10. ____ Penne
11. ____ Radiatori
12. ____ Spaghetti
13. ____ Tortellini
14. ____ Vermicelli

ENGLISH TRANSLATIONS

A. Worms
B. Butterflies
C. Cooking pot
D. Thin hair
E. Little faithful ones
F. Little strings
G. Little slices
H. Little beards
I. Little ears
J. Little pies
K. Little tongues
L. Radiator
M. Pens
N. Shells

1. **H.** Little beards (Barbina)

2. **D.** Thin hair (Capellini)

3. **N.** Shells (Conchiglie)

4. **B.** Butterflies (Farfalle)

5. **E.** Little faithful ones (Fedelini)

6. **G.** Little slices (Fettuccine)

7. **C.** Cooking pot (Lasagna)

8. **K.** Little tongues (Linguine)

9. **I.** Little ears (Orecchiette)

10. **M.** Pens (Penne)

11. **L.** Radiator (Radiatori)

12. **F.** Little strings (Spaghetti)

13. **J.** Little pies (Tortellini)

14. **A.** Worms (Vermicelli)

Legend has it that the eggy and creamy carbonara sauce we know today may have gotten its name from the Italian word for "charcoal burner's wife" or "coal miner's wife." This sauce paired with pasta might have been favored by charcoal workers because it's so rich and filling. I'd like my little tongues in charcoal sauce, please!

KAREN

HEY, WHERE'D YOU GET THAT CHEESE?

BY COLIN

When it comes to foodstuffs, few things are funnier than cheese. Thinking about it, talking about it—just saying the word "cheese"—brings a smile to your face. (As an added bonus, you can eat it.) But how well do you really know the world's most famous cheeses?

Can you tell me the country where each of these popular cheeses originated?

QUESTIONS

1. Golly, where'd you get that **Gouda**?

2. Girl, where'd you grab that **Gruyère**?

3. Listen, where'd you locate that **Limburger**?

4. Cool, where'd you cop that **Colby**?

5. Champ, where'd you chase down that **Cheddar**?

6. Buddy, where'd you buy that **Brie**?

7. Yo, where'd you yank that **Jarlsberg**?

8. Gee, where'd you grab that **Gorgonzola**?

9. Hey, where'd you happen upon that **Havarti**?

10. Man, where'd you get your mitts on that **Manchego**?

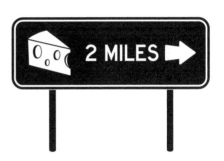

These stinky cheese puns are making me bleu.

CHRIS

Aw, a gouda pun curds all ills!

DANA

1. **The Netherlands**. Named after the city of Gouda, which was home to a thriving cheese marketplace where this type of cheese was traded as far back as the 12th century. In the old days, if you wanted some Gouda, you went to Gouda... and the name stuck.

2. **Switzerland**. Named after the town of Gruyères. Let's take a moment to show our respect for this easy-melting wonder cheese. Without it, we wouldn't have the greatest gift ever bestowed on cheese-lovers: Swiss fondue.

3. **Belgium**. Named after the former Duchy of Limburg, most of which is in modern-day Belgium. Limburger is generally regarded as the world's stinkiest cheese, with an aroma landing somewhere between sweaty boots and moldy feet. Enjoy!

4. **United States**. Named after the city of Colby in America's cheese heartland, Wisconsin. Along with Monterey Jack, this is one of the two most popular American-born cheeses (and no, Cheez Whiz doesn't count).

> I just want to whey in to say that this quiz is pretty legendairy. I want to Edam all. How did you do? Time to get grated on your answers.
>
> **KAREN**

5. **United Kingdom**. Named after the village of Cheddar in Somerset County, England. The classic orange hue we typically associate with this cheese isn't a naturally occurring attribute—it comes from annatto (achiote-seed coloring) added to the mixture. "White Cheddar" is simply made without annatto.

6. **France**. Named after the region of Brie. Although it's been popular in France for hundreds of years, Brie wasn't available in the U.S. until the 1930s, when the advent of refrigerated ocean liners finally allowed this soft cheese to survive a journey of more than a few days.

7. **Norway**. Named after the historic Jarlsberg territory. Unlike most cheese recipes, the exact formula for producing Jarlsberg is a closely guarded secret. I suspect the main ingredient is holes.

8. **Italy**. Named after the town of Gorgonzola near Milan. This cheese's distinctive blue mold comes from the same genus of fungi used to make penicillin. (Use cheese only as prescribed.)

9. **Denmark**. Named after Havarthigaard, a dairy farm near Copenhagen where this comparatively new cheese was created in the early 1900s.

10. **Spain**. Named after Manchega sheep, which provide the milk for the cheese. The sheep in turn are named for the La Mancha plains region. (Yes, the same La Mancha featured in Miguel de Cervantes's classic *Don Quixote*!)

Did you do well? Celebrate with some cheese! Did you fare poorly? Drown your sorrows in some cheese.

ANIMAL SECRETION SPOTLIGHT: BEAVER BUTT JUICE

BY KAREN

Hands down, this is probably the most popular and talked-about fact we've ever shared on the show. It's the triumvirate of our favorite types of trivia: animals, food, and butts. It also cemented the beaver's rightful place as the official *Good Job, Brain!* spokesanimal.

Beavers are amazing animals: they use their orange teeth (colored by the natural iron compound in the enamel) to chop down wood and build elaborate dams, and within their nether regions they produce a secretion that's used for a super-weird purpose. Though we like the casual ring of "beaver butt juice," let's get technical and use the actual term for this animal secretion: *castoreum*. Both male and female adult beavers have castor sacs at the base of their tails near their butt holes, and these sacs produce castoreum, a smelly brown substance that beavers use for scent and territory marking.

And...you've probably eaten it.

Castoreum most notably is used to enhance vanilla- and raspberry-flavored foods. In its raw form, castoreum initially probably smells like what you think animal butts would smell like. But after mellowing out and being processed (usually in alcohol tinctures), what's left is a substance that smells leathery, wild, smoky, and vanilla-sweet, thanks to the beaver's unique plant diet. The substance is nontoxic and deemed "generally recognized as safe" by the Food and Drug Administration, and most importantly, it's classified as a type of natural flavoring.[24] And just think how often you've seen "natural flavorings" on food packaging.

Well, how did someone find out about this?! Oh man, I wish I knew. I imagine there was this one guy (most likely a fur trapper from the 1800s) who wedged his nose between the furry butt cheeks of a beaver butt, took a giant whiff, and was like, *"Hey, you know, after parsing out the pee and poo smell, this stuff reminds me of vanilla! I'm going to put it in my next Bundt cake recipe just in time for Earl's retirement party."* History has taught us that for centuries, people have been using various animal secretions (like whale vomit and deer musk) as perfume additives, so in a way, anal beaver juice is not *that* weird.

Getting castoreum is not an easy process. It can be humanely harvested (by getting hold of a beaver and "milking" its butt), but the amount of output probably doesn't justify the messy and annoying procedure. Thanks to modern innovations in food science, most flavorings can be synthetically reproduced, and real vanillin is more readily available than castoreum. So castoreum consumption is rather small—only about 292 pounds yearly.[25] There might not be any beaver butt juice in that dollar pack of mass-produced vanilla wafers from the supermarket, but who's to say castoreum didn't make its way into something else you've eaten in your lifetime?

The moral of the story? Keep smelling those animal butts. Be that mythical guy who decided to take a chance on a beaver, and change the world.

24. G. A. Burdock, "Safety assessment of castoreum extract as a food ingredient," *International Journal of Toxicology* 26, no. 1 (Jan-Feb 2007): 51-5.

25. George Burdock, *Fenaroli's Handbook of Flavor Ingredients,* 5th ed. (Boca Raton, FL: CRC Press, 2004).

TRUTH IN ADVERTISING

BY CHRIS

Here are abbreviated biographies of faces you see peering down on you from various mass-produced food products. The catch is that some of these are real biographies of actual people pictured on the food packaging, and some are totally made up, by me, because the people on the boxes are fictional characters. Can you tell the real from the fake?

REAL OR FAKE?

1. Born in Indiana, Orville Redenbacher studied agriculture and personally developed the hybrid corn that he would use for his explosively popular popcorn.

2. Jemima Green ran a small-town South Carolina diner, but she was best known for her muffins, not her pancakes. When she sold the "Aunt Jemima" brand to Quaker Oats, it was the ready-made pancake mix that busy suburban moms loved best, and the muffin mix was quickly discontinued.

3. When his brother Arthur McDonald came up with the idea of having kids' entertainment at their hamburger stand, Ronald McDonald decided to come to work dressed as a clown. It was a huge hit and became a staple in their later television commercials (although no longer played by the successful company founder).

4. Ben, whose last name has been lost to history, was a farmer from Houston, Texas, well known for growing exceptional, high-quality rice. They named the Uncle Ben's rice brand after him (although that's not his picture on the cover).

5. Living in England, Joy Masterson hardly ever ate maple syrup. But she fell in love with an American soldier named Frank Butterworth and returned with him to his home state of Vermont, where he ate pancakes with syrup almost every day. Ever economical, the newlywed Mrs. Butterworth perfected a recipe for homemade syrup, and the rest is history.

6. The husband-and-wife founders of McKee Foods wanted a mascot to put on the boxes of their sugar-stuffed snack cakes, and they looked no further than their granddaughter Deborah, calling the line "Little Debbie" and sticking her smiling face on every box.

7. Academy Award–winning actor Paul Newman was also something of a chef, and he and a friend often whipped up homemade salad dressing and gave it out as gifts. A lifelong philanthropist, he founded the "Newman's Own" food brand with the intent of donating all the profits to charity.

8. Betty Crocker was no homemaker—she was a home economist who earned a degree from the University of Minnesota and went to work for local food powerhouse General Mills.

9. Dave Thomas was a successful Kentucky Fried Chicken franchise owner who sold his restaurants back to Colonel Harland Sanders, then invested that money in a hamburger chain. For a mascot, he chose his daughter, whose nickname was "Wendy."

10. Ettore Boiardi immigrated from Italy in the early 20th century, eventually opening an Italian restaurant in Cleveland. When he decided to put his spaghetti sauce in cans and sell it around the country, he named the product "Chef Boy-Ar-Dee" so that people could pronounce it easily.

1. **True**. Orville was real, and this is his real story.

2. **Fake**. Sorry, Aunt Jemima is a made-up character.

3. **Fake**. As wonderful as this would be, I made it up. (McDonald's was indeed founded by two brothers, but their names were Richard and Maurice.)

4. **True**. Ben was real, although the guy on the box of "Uncle Ben's" instant rice is actually a Chicago chef named Frank Brown.

5. **Fake**. Mrs. Butterworth is a sentient, talking syrup bottle. (But her first name *is* Joy.)

6. **True**. McKee Foods also owns "Drake's Cakes."

7. **True**. Yes, Paul Newman was a real person.

8. **Fake**. Betty Crocker is an invention, but this is the real biography of Marjorie Husted, who helped create the character.

9. **True**. Wendy is real (and so, for that matter, was Colonel Sanders).

10. **True**. The company eventually dropped the hyphens from the name.

UM, ACTUALLY: FOOD EDITION

BY CHRIS

I love to cook, and I love learning about cooking—all the little tricks and techniques you can use to make your food not undelicious. Many of us have a lifetime of received wisdom in this area, cooking know-how we've learned from our parents, who learned it from their parents, who learned it who-knows-where. But some of these cooking tips turn out to be myths—or at least, we're not doing them for the right reasons.

"SALTING THE PASTA WATER MAKES THE SPAGHETTI COOK FASTER."

This is one of those tricky myths, because it's technically, mathematically, scientifically true—but not enough to make any difference, and it's not the actual reason you do it. Adding salt to water does raise the boiling point of water, yes. But you'd have to add *half a pound* of salt per quart of water to raise the boiling point by just 2 degrees Celsius/ 3.6 degrees Fahrenheit.[26] So that pinch of salt in your giant pot of pasta isn't affecting the boiling point to any significant degree.

But once my pasta water gets boiling, I always dump a generous amount of salt into it— enough so that it tastes basically like the ocean. Why? Because salt tastes good, and when you're cooking dry pasta in salt water, salt is absorbed into the pasta along with water, making the pasta taste better. (Don't worry, most of the salt gets dumped out with the water afterward.)

So yes, you do want to salt the pasta water—but *after* it's boiled.

"IF YOU PUT WINE INTO A DISH, ALL THE ALCOHOL EVAPORATES."

"Oh, don't worry—all the alcohol cooks out!" says Aunt Lou merrily, as she glug-glugs a bottle of red table wine into her patented tomato gravy. Is she right, or is the phrase "hitting the sauce" about to get a whole new meaning?

---

26. Anne Marie Helmenstine, "Why Do You Add Salt to Boiling Water?" About Education, updated March 27, 2016, accessed July 14, 2016, http://chemistry.about.com/od/foodcookingchemistry/f/Why-Do-You-Add-Salt-To-Boiling-Water.htm.

It's certainly the case that applying heat to alcohol will cause some of it to start evaporating. But I'd always heard that all the alcohol, or at least the vast majority, will be gone from the final dish after any significant cooking time. The United States Department of Agriculture studied this, and the answer in a nutshell is *heck no.*

How much alcohol is left depends on the style, temperature, and duration of cooking—and it's probably a lot more than you think. If you do a flambé (pouring spirits into a pan and setting the contents on fire), you'll actually leave behind about 75 percent of the alcohol! If you pour wine into your spaghetti sauce and simmer it for an hour, 25 percent of the alcohol will still be in there. Another hour and you're down to 10 percent, which still isn't zero.[27]

So if you're avoiding alcohol entirely, you probably shouldn't eat anything that uses alcohol at any step of the recipe.

"PUTTING AVOCADO PIT INTO GUACAMOLE KEEPS IT FROM TURNING BROWN."

As if the pit of the avocado possessed some magical property! Sure, this works, but only on the guacamole that the pit's surface touches. Contact with the air turns guacamole brown and gross-tasting (it's safe to eat, but you wouldn't want to). If you want to keep your tortilla dip fresh and green, push plastic wrap tightly against it or carefully cover it with a thin layer of water before you fridge it.

"PORK HAS TO BE COOKED WELL-DONE."

Trichinosis is not something that you want, unless you want your body to be home to a colony of tiny little roundworms. Trichinosis parasites can infect pigs, and since they're inside the meat, you have to cook pork all the way to a dusty gray, well-done temperature, right?

Wrong, according to the USDA. You can have your pork nice and pink inside, at 145 degrees Fahrenheit (the same recommended standard as for beef).[28] Thanks to improved farming standards, trichinosis parasites are basically not an issue anymore when buying pork in

27. "USDA Table of Nutrient Retention Factors," Nutrient Data Laboratory, Beltsville Human Nutrition Research Center, Agricultural Research Service, U.S. Department of Agriculture, published December 2007, accessed July 14, 2016, www.ars .usda.gov/SP2UserFiles/Place/12354500/Date/retn/retn06.pdf.

28. Cindy Cunningham, "New USDA Guidelines Lower Pork Cooking Temperature," National Park Board, published May 24, 2011, accessed July 14, 2016, www.pork.org/new-usda-guidelines-lower-pork-cooking-temperature.

the U.S. The Centers for Disease Control says only about 20 people a year in the U.S. get trichinosis, and the large majority of those get it from eating wild game, not pigs.

"WASHING MUSHROOMS TOUGHENS THEM UP AND RUINS THEM."

When you start watching food television, one of those expert-level cooking tips you hear early on is that you shouldn't wash mushrooms, but instead lightly scrape off the dirt with a brush or paper towel. This is because mushrooms are highly absorbent, and they'll soak up water and lose their consistency.

But man, having to sit there and individually brush the dirt off every single button mushroom is a real pain in the butt. Surely it wouldn't hurt to just run them under the faucet real fast, right? Right. While you certainly shouldn't leave your mushrooms soaking in water, if you just rinse them in running water for the two seconds it'll take to wash off the dirt, you're not going to hurt anything. (Although this only applies to mushrooms like buttons or portobellos, not wild mushrooms—those apparently get pretty gross in water.)[29]

29. Danielle Walsh, "5 Common Mushroom Cooking Mistakes, and How to Avoid Them," *Bon Appétit*, published April 30, 2014, accessed July 14, 2016, www.bonappetit.com/test-kitchen/common-mistakes/article/mushroom-common-mistakes.

A BALTHAZAR FOR THE TABLE, PLEASE!

BY DANA

Have you ever seen a comically large bottle of Champagne and just assumed it was some sort of novelty prop? It probably wasn't! There's actually an array of outsize Champagne bottles named for Biblical kings or historical figures (mostly). Being familiar with the names of these bottles can come in handy for trivia contests and impressing your exceptionally fancy friends.

1 BOTTLE (0.75 L)

2 BOTTLES (1.5 L) = **Magnum**, shortened from *magnum bonum*, which means "large good" in Latin

4 BOTTLES (3 L) = **Jeroboam**, named for the biblical king

6 BOTTLES (4.5 L) = **Rehoboam**, named for the biblical king

8 BOTTLES (6 L) = **Methuselah**, named after the Bible's oldest man

12 BOTTLES (9 L) = **Salmanazar**, named for the biblical king

16 BOTTLES (12 L) = **Balthazar**, named for the biblical figure

20 BOTTLES (15 L) = **Nebuchadnezzar**, named for the biblical king

24 BOTTLES (18 L) = **Solomon**, named for the biblical king

35 BOTTLES (26 L) = **Sovereign**, named for the ship *Sovereign of the Seas*

36 BOTTLES (27 L) = **Primat**, probably related to *primus*, which means "the first" in Latin

40 BOTTLES (30 L) = **Melchizedek**, named for the biblical king

WORD NERDERY

WE LOVE US SOME LANGUAGE,

SO HERE ARE THE WORDS,
PHRASES, LETTERS, MARKS
WE FIND THE MOST FASCINATING.

HEY, LET'S ACTUALLY USE LATIN CORRECTLY!

BY CHRIS

I enjoy dropping Latin phrases and abbreviations—e.g., *sic*, et cetera—into things that I'm writing, not because I'm a nerd *per se* but because I'm a pretentious word nerd. But when we get a little overenthusiastic with our Latin and misuse the phrases, the resulting sentences can be suboptimal—i.e., incorrect. Let's get our Latin straight.

e.g.

An abbreviation of *exempli gratia*, this can be dropped in when you would otherwise say "for example."

Ex. "Sweden has many kinds of gross candy, e.g., salty licorice."

i.e.

An abbreviation of *id est*, this substitutes for "that is."

Ex. "Castoreum comes from a beaver's nether regions, i.e., the butt."

sic

While it's often found printed after misspelled words, *sic* is not an abbreviation of "spelled incorrectly." *Sic* just means "thus," and it's an abbreviation of *sic erat scriptum*, or "thus it was written."

What that means is that when you're copying something someone else wrote, you put a *sic* in there to indicate that an error or intentionally odd spelling was present in the original text, and it is not your error.

Ex. "In 1992, Vice President Dan Quayle botched a spelling bee when he told a student the word was spelled *potatoe* [*sic*]."

n.b.

An abbreviation of *nota bene*, or "note well," this is used by a writer to indicate that the reader should pay attention to the following, or to point out a side comment.

N.b.: I first encountered *sic* in a book about Nintendo games. The author had used it to reference an enemy named "Albatoss," to indicate that it was not the author's misspelling of "Albatross" but an intentionally punny name.

ergo

Ergo means "therefore," and it joins up a cause and an effect.

Ex. "Phyllis thought the lyrics to 'The First Noel' were 'Barney's the King of Israel'; *ergo*, she was quite embarrassed at the Christmas sing-a-long."

per se

Perhaps the most misused and abused Latin phrase, *per se* is used today to mean almost anything except what it actually means: "by itself."

Ex. "I'm not scared of clowns *per se*; but I'm scared of clowns wearing miniskirts."

et cetera

This means "and others"—note that when spelled out, it's two words. It can be abbreviated "etc." But did you know that since the ampersand is actually a ligature of the letters E and T, you can also abbreviate it "&c."? Try it on your friends!

N.b.: Why's it called an "ampersand"? Well, they used to put this character at the end of the English-language alphabet, as the 27th "letter" after the Z. So when you recited the alphabet, you'd finish by saying, "W, X, Y, Z, and, *per se*, and"— i.e., "and, by itself, and." It didn't take inattentive children very long to slur that into "ampersand."

BACK TALK

BY DANA

Below are clues for words and phrases that contain the word "back." Fill in the blanks and then arrange the boxed letters to reveal the answer to the final clue.

CLUES

1. A kind of bacon: __ ☐ __ __ __ __ __

2. The vast, remote, arid area of Australia: ☐ __ __ __ __ __ __

3. To mark or supply with a date that is earlier than the actual date:
   __ __ __ __ ☐ __ __ __

4. An insult disguised as a compliment: __ __ __ __ __ __ ☐ __ __ __

5. A Major League Baseball team from Arizona:
   __ __ __ ☐ __ __ __ __ __ __ __

6. A currency used during the American Civil War:
   ☐ __ __ __ __ __ __ __ __

7. Quasimodo from Victor Hugo's masterpiece: __ __ ☐ __ __ __ __ __ __

8. A feral pig or wild boar in North America: __ ☐ __ __ __ __ __ __ __

9. An old-timey easy chair: __ __ ☐ __ __ __ __ __

10. To move bike gears in reverse: __ __ __ __ __ __ __ ☐ __

11. A piece of excavating equipment: __ __ __ __ __ __ ☐

12. To ride without a saddle: ☐ __ __ __ __ __ __ __

13. The Volkswagen Golf, for example: ___ ___ [ ] ___ ___ ___ ___ ___ ___

14. A style of clothing with straps that form a V or T pattern between the shoulder blades:

___ ___ [ ] ___ ___ ___ ___ ___

15. A shoe held on by a strap across the heel: ___ ___ [ ] ___ ___ ___ ___ ___ ___

16. A species of baleen whale: ___ [ ] ___ ___ ___ ___ ___ ___

17. A dog breed developed in a country now known as Zimbabwe:

___ ___ [ ] ___ ___ ___ ___ ___   ___ ___ ___ ___ ___ ___ ___ ___

18. A freshwater fish with a distinctive dorsal fin:

[ ] ___ ___ ___ ___ ___ ___

19. The Internet Archive's Digital Collection:

___ ___ [ ] ___ ___ ___   ___ ___ ___ ___ ___ ___

20. The recoil or rebound from a gun: [ ] ___ ___ ___ ___ ___ ___ ___

21. One of the oldest known board games: ___ ___ ___ ___ ___ ___ [ ] ___ ___ ___

22. Title of a 1966 Beatles song:

___ ___ ___ ___ [ ] ___ ___ ___   ___ [ ] ___ ___ ___ [ ]

Unscramble the boxed letters to reveal the answer to the clue below.

Final clue: One who second guesses.

Boxed letters:

___ ___ ___ ___ ___ ___ ___ ___ ___ ___ ___ ___ ___ ___ ___ ___ ___ ___ ___ ___

FINAL ANSWER:

___ ___ ___ ___ ___ ___ ___ ___ ___ ___ ___ ___ ___ ___ ___ ___ ___ ___

1. F**A**TBACK
2. **O**UTBACK
3. BACK**D**ATE
4. BACKHA**N**DED
5. DIA**M**ONDBACK
6. **G**REENBACKS
7. HU**N**CHBACK
8. R**A**ZORBACK
9. WI**N**GBACK
10. BACKPED**A**L
11. BACKHO**E**

12. **B**AREBACK
13. HA**T**CHBACK
14. RA**C**ERBACK
15. SL**I**NGBACK
16. H**U**MPBACK
17. RH**O**DESIAN RIDGEBACK
18. **Q**UILLBACK
19. WA**Y**BACK MACHINE
20. **K**ICKBACK
21. BACKGA**MM**ON
22. PAPE**R**BACK W**RITE**R

FINAL ANSWER: The boxed letters rearrange to form "one who guesses," a MONDAY MORNING QUARTERBACK

WHO, WHAT, OR WHERE?

BY COLIN

You could probably guess that Champagne is named after something French. But was *Champagne* a person? Or perhaps a place? Trivia nerds demand answers![30] To help you learn your famous (and not-so-famous) namesakes, this challenging quiz is all about things named after other things. Some you may know, some you can probably guess, and some… well, you can always make up funny answers if nothing else. Good luck!

QUESTIONS

1. Who, what, or where is **Kobe beef** named after?

2. Who, what, or where is the **diesel engine** named after?

3. Who, what, or where is the **Caesar salad** named after?

4. Who, what, or where is the **torpedo** named after?

5. Who, what, or where is the **emery board** named after?

6. Who, what, or where is **shrapnel** named after?

7. Who, what, or where is **Epsom salt** named after?

8. Who, what, or where is the **color magenta** named after?

---

30. Champagne takes its name from the Champagne region of France, famous for producing sparkling white wine.

1. Kobe beef, famous for its tender texture and fine marbling, is named after the city of **Kobe, Japan**. Among other restrictions, true Kobe beef can only come from cattle that were born and raised in Hyōgo Prefecture, of which Kobe is the capital.

2. The diesel engine is named after **Rudolf Diesel**, a German inventor who obtained one of the earliest patents for a compression-ignition engine, in the 1890s. (A diesel engine ignites fuel using compression-generated heat, in contrast to a gasoline engine, which ignites an air-fuel mixture using spark plugs.)

3. The Caesar salad is named for restaurateur **Caesar Cardini**. The exact circumstances surrounding the first Caesar salad are a little unclear, but according to the "official" story (as told by Cardini's daughter), it was born during an unexpected rush at one of Caesar Cardini's restaurants on the Fourth of July, 1924. With limited ingredients available, Cardini had to make do with whatever was at hand. So he improvised a savory romaine-based salad similar to what we know today as a Caesar, and it was a hit! (Complicating this version of the story is the fact that more than one of his chefs would later claim to have invented the recipe. At any rate, none other than Julia Child herself specifically mentioned in one of her books that she had eaten a Caesar Salad at one of Cardini's restaurants when she was a girl in the 1920s.)

4. The torpedo takes its name from fish in the **genus *Torpedo***: round, flat electric rays known for their numbing shock. Early torpedo weapons were somewhat crude devices, often just bundles of explosives attached to the ends of long poles or towed behind vessels. The name is an allusion to the unpleasant surprise awaiting someone unlucky enough to cross paths with an angry *Torpedo* ray.

5. Emery is the **gritty rock material** that coats an emery board. It consists primarily of corundum, or aluminum oxide in crystal form. Corundum is a fairly

common, naturally transparent mineral, but some of its alternate forms are valued as gemstones. When it has iron impurities, it appears blue/green and is called a sapphire; when it has chromium impurities, it takes on a lustrous red hue and is called a ruby!

6. Shrapnel is named after **Henry Shrapnel**, a British army officer in the late 1700s. As a lieutenant in the Royal Artillery regiment, Shrapnel devised a new type of fragmentation shell with a time-delayed explosion. Earlier fragmentation shells worked somewhat like giant shotgun shells, limiting their effective range on the battlefield. But the new "Shrapnel shell" could be fired like a standard artillery round, only exploding in a hail of deadly shot once it was close to the enemy. Today *shrapnel* generally means any type of small fragments blown out from an explosion.

7. Epsom salt (or salts) is named after the **town of Epsom in Surrey, England**. As far back as the 17th century, Epsom was known for the rejuvenating properties of its mineral-rich spring water, which could be boiled down to obtain natural magnesium sulfate. The crystalline magnesium sulfate was known as Epsom salt (sometimes called English salt outside of the region) and was dissolved in baths to soothe tired muscles, much as it is today.

8. The color "magenta" is named after the city of **Magenta, Italy**—albeit somewhat indirectly. In 1859, French chemist François-Emmanuel Verguin developed an artificial purplish-reddish dye he named *fuchsin* after its similarity to the color of fuchsia blossoms. At that time, France was fighting in the Second Italian War of Independence, and after a decisive military victory by Napoleon III at the Battle of Magenta, Verguin renamed his dye *magenta* in honor of the victory.

OUR FAVORITE EGGCORNS

BY THE WHOLE GANG

"It's a moo point," Joey once said in a 2000 episode of *Friends*. "You know, like a cow's opinion. It doesn't matter." Three years later, linguistics professor Geoffrey Pullum gave us a word to use for these misheard phrases: "eggcorn," after a woman who thought that the acorns she found on the ground were called "eggcorns" because, well, they look like little eggs or corn kernels.

As opposed to the simple misuse of a word, with an eggcorn there's often a semi-reasonable explanation for the mistake. It makes sense that someone who hears that Grandma has "Alzheimer's disease" might think that she has "old-timer's disease." Sometimes it's because the real word is unfamiliar to the listener (like "moot" for Joey) or has fallen out of common use. (Sometimes the eggcorn makes more sense, if you ask us.)

Some of these new words and phrases are very common—even to the point of replacing the originals! Some we've seen only once. But they're all eggcorns, and we love them. Here are some of our favorites. (And in case you can't figure it out, the eggcorn comes first.)

- Pre-Madonna (prima donna)
- A doggy-dog world (a dog-eat-dog world)
- A blessing in the skies (a blessing in disguise)
- For all intensive purposes (for all intents and purposes)
- A sick sense (a sixth sense)
- Mating name (maiden name)
- The best thing since life's bread (the best thing since sliced bread)
- Chicken spots (chicken pox)
- Cigarette buds (cigarette butts)
- Sugar code (sugar-coat)
- Biting my time (biding my time)
- Old wise tale (old wives' tale)
- Scandally clad (scantily clad)
- Very close veins (varicose veins)
- Self phone (cell phone)
- Quarter Roy pants (corduroy pants)
- Coldslaw (cole slaw)
- By a hare's breath (by a hair's breadth)
- A poseable thumb (opposable thumb)
- In lame man's terms (in layman's terms)
- Card shark (card sharp)
- Statue of limitations (statute of limitations)
- Another thing coming (another think coming)
- Antidotal evidence (anecdotal evidence)
- Die of beaties (diabetes)
- Ex-patriot (expatriate)
- Never regions (nether regions)
- Plate mat (place mat)
- Expresso (espresso)
- Pee-ons (peons)
- Play it by year (play it by ear)
- The feeble position (the fetal position)
- Mindgrain headache (migraine headache)

MIND CRUNCHER

BY CHRIS

Here's a pencil-and-paper puzzle for you! The answers to these questions all have something in common. Enter each one into the grid, one letter per space, as you figure them out (it's okay to Google if no one is watching you). The letters that land in the boxes will spell out one last clue, for one final answer.

CLUES

1. Stanley Kirk Burrell's alias: ___ ___ ___ ☐ ___ ___ ___ ___

2. Rainier Wolfcastle's defining role: ___ ___ ☐ ___ ___ ___

3. Patrick Dempsey character, familiarly: ___ ___ ☐ ___ ___ ___ ___ ___

4. Challenger casualty: ___ ___ ___ ☐ ___ ___ ___ ___

5. Failed diet entrée from #6: ___ ___ ___ ___ ___ ___ ___ ___ ☐ ___ ___

6. Fast-food eatery: ___ ___ ___ ___ ___ ___ ___ ___ , ☐

7. Orlando airport (abbr.): ___ ___ ☐

8. Failed Italian entrée from #6: ___ ___ ☐ ___ ___ ___ ___

9. Annual home of Chicago Auto Show:

___ ___ ___ ___ ___ ___ ___ ___ ___ ☐ ___ ___ ___

10. Irascible tennis player: ___ ___ ___ ___ ___ □ ___

11. Relativity artist: ___   ___   ___ □ ___ ___ ___ ___

12. 2011 U.S. Open victor: ___ ___ □ ___ ___ ___ ___

13. Senator with a list of names: ___ ___ ___ ___ ___ □ ___ ___

14. Spawned Spawn: ___ ___ ___ ___ ___ ___ ___ □

FINAL ANSWER: ___ ___   ___ ___ ___ ___   ___ ___ ___

Every answer in this puzzle begins with the letters MC.

1. MC H**A**MMER

2. MC**B**AIN

3. MC**D**REAMY

4. (Christa) MCA**UL**IFFE

5. MCLEAN DE**L**UXE

6. MCDONALD'**S**

7. MC**O**

8. MC**P**IZZA

9. MCCORMICK **P**LACE

10. (John) MCENR**OE**

11. M.C. E**S**CHER

12. (Rory) MCI**L**ROY

13. (Joe) MCCAR**T**HY

14. (Todd) MCFARLAN**E**

FINAL ANSWER: When the boxed letters are read in order, they spell ABDUL'S OPPOSITE. This should lead you to Paula Abdul's duet partner in the unforgettable 1988 song "Opposites Attract"—whose name was (of course) MC SKAT KAT. Like McPizza, he's an enduring icon of the 1980s.

I FORGOT WHAT I WAS SUPPOSED TO REMEMBER

BY CHRIS

Mnemonics! They're handy linguistic devices that help you to memorize things you need to remember! For example: the mnemonic HOMES helps you remember the Great Lakes (Huron, Ontario, Michigan, Erie, Superior).

My problem today is this: I remember all these mnemonics but I can't remember what they're supposed to help me remember. Can you help? Check out these mnemonics and try to figure out what exactly it is I'm trying to keep straight in my head. I remember this much, at least: all of these have something to do with mathematics...somehow.

MNEMONICS

1. Please excuse my dear Aunt Sally.

2. King Henry died by drinking chocolate milk.

3. Nice doggy!

4. I value xylophones like cows dig milk.

5. Some old hippie caught another hippie tripping on acid.

6. A rat in the house may eat the ice cream.

7. May I have a large container of coffee?

1. Oh, right, I was trying to remember the **order of operations** for doing a math problem: parentheses, exponents, multiplication, division, addition, subtraction.

2. Ah, of course; it's the **metric system multipliers**: kilo, hecto, deca, base, deci, centi, and milli.

3. This one's great for kids learning fractions: **numerator and denominator**, the numbers on the top and bottom of the division line.

4. I, V, X, L, C, D, and M are—how could I forget?—the **seven Roman numerals** in order: 1, 5, 10, 50, 100, 500, and 1,000.

> In music class they taught us "Every Good Boy Does Fine" as a way to remember the notes on the lines of sheet music (E-G-B-D-F). Years later, I learned other kids were taught "Every Good Boy Deserves Fudge" and felt I'd been cheated.
>
> **COLIN**

5. SOH CAH TOA, for trigonometry students, helps you remember the **calculations to find the values for the sine** (opposite/hypotenuse), **cosine** (adjacent over hypotenuse), and **tangent** (opposite/adjacent). (Although honestly I just imagine someone soaking their toe.)

6. I hope you didn't spend a lot of time trying to figure out what mathematical formula is suggested by this mnemonic; it's just here to help me remember how to spell **ARITHMETIC**.

7. Hey, I never said that all of these were acronyms! The first letter in each of these words will get you absolutely nowhere, but if you count the *number* of letters in each word, you can see they spell out the **numerical constant pi** to seven places—3.1415927.

I MUSTACHE YOU A QUESTION: THE *GOOD JOB, BRAIN!* CROSSWORD

It's not easy to do a crossword puzzle on a podcast. In fact, it's nearly impossible. Thinking about it some more, it's *totally* impossible. But thanks to *Good Job, Brain!* superfan Neville Fogarty (whose crosswords have appeared in the *New York Times*, *Los Angeles Times*, and elsewhere), we finally have a crossword of our own! Enjoy!

ACROSS

1. United ___ Emirates
5. Scott who voiced Baymax in *Big Hero 6*
10. Georgetown athlete
14. State bird of the Aloha State
15. Croc's relative
16. Locker room nuisance
17. *Fly Away Home* actress
19. Surfer's concern
20. Dred Scott, notably
21. Liverpool and Dublin are on it
23. Football phenom Manning
25. Hexagonal state
26. He plays Thor on the silver screen
33. Start of a conclusion
34. One of the Bobbsey twins
35. *Yoshi's* ___ (Nintendo 64 game with a Super Happy Tree)
36. Set one's sights
37. On the line
40. "You betcha"
41. Nose-in-the-air folks
43. Gauntlet character
44. Frozen drink brand
45. "We've Only Just Begun" vocalist
49. Bert who played the Cowardly Lion
50. Last mo. of the yr.
51. Fashion trend of 2010
55. Large South American birds
59. Tibetan creature... maybe
60. Best Actor Oscar winner of the 83rd Annual Academy Awards (held in 2011)
62. Caesarean accusation
63. Animal with a spitting image?
64. Cartoon Network: Adult Swim :: Nickelodeon : Nick at ___
65. Baseball feature

66. Money in the music industry

67. Actress Rowlands of *The Notebook*

DOWN

1. "No ifs, ___, or buts!"

2. Not imaginary

3. *Frozen* sister

4. Animals that produce castoreum with glands in their butts

5. Get older

6. *The Persistence of Memory* painter

7. Sirius, for example

8. Thorium-230

9. Meetings at the No-Tell Motel

10. "Pop quiz, ___" (memorable *Speed* line)

11. Garfield's companion

12. "When 900 years old you reach, look as good you will not" speaker

13. "We ___ Young" (#1 hit for the band fun)

18. Place to order a ham and cheese sandwich

22. Hole for an anchor cable

24. Ain't right?

26. Country that, despite its width, follows a single time zone

27. Phlegm or black bile, for example

28. Controls

29. Keyboard button next to the apostrophe

30. Word that can follow "Rolls" or "Rose"

31. More loyal

32. ___ train (anticipation surrounding the release of a new video game)

33. Item on a to-do list

37. Hit ___ (run into trouble)

38. Austrian peak

39. Rapper known for his marriage to Britney Spears

42. Where the Smurfs come from

44. Needing a scratch

46. Chewing gum ingredient

47. Former Governator Schwarzenegger

48. Toy line known for its projectiles

51. Ballet leap

52. Jazz singer James

53. Really happy

54. ___ Valley, California

56. One of the Great Lakes

57. Business letter abbr.

58. Stadium where the Mets used to play

59. Response to a correct answer

61. Scottish refusal

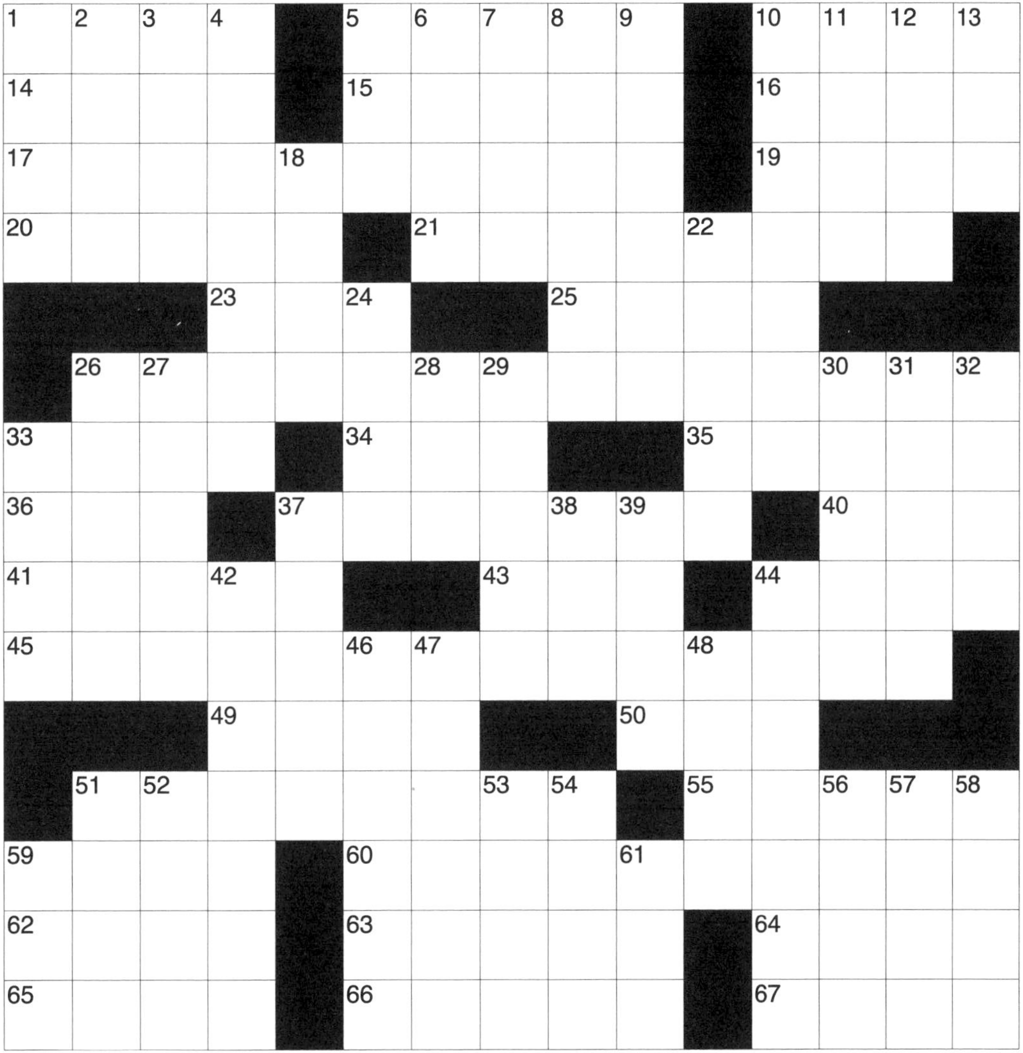

ACROSS

5. Adsit	23. Eli	40. Yup	55. Rheas
10. Hoya	25. Utah	41. Snobs	59. Yeti
14. Nene	26. Chris	43. Elf	60. Colin Firth
15. Gator	Hemsworth	44. Icee	62. Ettu
16. Odor	33. Thus	45. Karen	63. Llama
17. Dan Adelany	34. Nan	Carpenter	64. Nite
19. Tide	35. Story	49. Lahr	65. Seam
20. Slave	36. Aim	50. Dec.	66. Eddie
21. Irish Sea	37. At stake	51. Jeggings	67. Gena

DOWN

1. Ands	12. Yoda	32. Hype	52. Etta
2. Real	13. Are	33. Task	53. Glad
3. Anna	18. Deli	37. A snag	54. Simi
4. Beavers	22. Hawse	38. Alp	56. Erie
5. Age	24. Isn't	39. K Fed	57. Attn.
6. Dali	26. China	42. Belgium	58. Shea
7. Star	27. Humor	44. Itching	59. Yes
8. Ionium	28. Has	46. Chicle	61. Nae
9. Trysts	29. Enter	47. Arnold	
10. Hot shot	30. Royce	48. Nerf	
11. Odie	31. Truer	51. Jete	

Crossword solution grid:

1A	2R	3A	4B	■	5A	6D	7S	8I	9T	■	10H	11O	12Y	13A
14N	E	N	E	■	15G	A	T	O	R	■	16O	D	O	R
17D	A	N	A	18D	E	L	A	N	Y	■	19T	I	D	E
20S	L	A	V	E	■	21I	R	I	S	22H	S	E	A	■
■	■	23E	L	I	24	■	25U	T	A	H	■	■	■	■
■	26C	27H	R	I	S	28H	E	29M	S	W	O	30R	31T	32H
33T	H	U	S	■	34N	A	N	■	35S	T	O	R	Y	
36A	I	M	■	37A	T	S	T	38A	39K	E	■	40Y	U	P
41S	N	O	42B	S	■	43E	L	F	■	44I	C	E	E	■
45K	A	R	E	N	46C	47A	R	P	E	48N	T	E	R	■
■	■	■	49L	A	H	R	■	50D	E	C	■	■	■	■
■	51J	52E	G	G	I	N	53G	54S	■	55R	H	56E	57A	58S
59Y	E	T	I	■	60C	O	L	I	61N	F	I	R	T	H
62E	T	T	U	■	63L	L	A	M	A	■	64N	I	T	E
65S	E	A	M	■	66E	D	D	I	E	■	67G	E	N	A

FORTUNE-TELLING FOR DUMMIES

BY DANA

When I was 13, I really got into palmistry. I thought reading the future from the lines and whorls of our hands would be an amazing skill to cultivate. I read a bunch of books, memorized all the palmistry charts, and started practicing on my friends. Some of my predictions came true. Am I saying I was a gifted reader? Eh, probably not. But I'm not the only one who's looked for supernatural insight into the future. Below are the names of some divination methods. Can you match these names with the correct fortune-telling method?

NAMES

1. ____ Aeromancy

2. ____ Ambulomancy

3. ____ Arithmancy

4. ____ Astragalomancy

5. ____ Belomancy

6. ____ Bibliomancy

7. ____ Botanomancy

8. ____ Cartomancy

9. ____ Chiromancy

10. ____ Gastromancy

11. ____ Graptomancy

12. ____ Lecanomancy

13. ____ Metopomancy

14. ____ Onomancy

15. ____ Ornithomancy

16. ____ Pedomancy

17. ____ Pyromancy

18. ____ Scatomancy

19. ____ Tyromancy

20. ____ Zoomancy

MEANS OF DIVINATION

A. Actions of animals

B. Air, things in the air (clouds, birds, etc.), or the weather

C. Arrows

D. Bellies

E. Bird flight or bird cries

F. Books

G. Cheese

H. Dice or knucklebones

I. Faces or foreheads

J. Feet, especially the soles

K. Finger-rings

L. Fire

M. Hands

N. Handwriting

O. Names

P. Numbers

Q. Plants

R. Playing cards

S. Poop

T. Walking

U. Water in a basin

1. **B.** Air, things in the air (clouds, birds, etc.), or the weather (Aeromancy)

2. **T.** Walking (Ambulomancy)

3. **P.** Numbers (Arithmancy)

4. **H.** Dice or knucklebones (Astragalomancy)

5. **C.** Arrows (Belomancy)

6. **F.** Books (Bibliomancy)

7. **Q.** Plants (Botanomancy)

8. **R.** Playing Cards (Cartomancy)

9. **M.** Hands (Chiromancy)

10. **D.** Belly (Gastromancy)

11. **N.** Handwriting (Graptomancy)

12. **U.** Water in a basin (Lecanomancy)

13. **I.** Face or forehead (Metopomancy)

14. **O.** Names (Onomancy)

15. **E.** Birds (Ornithomancy)

16. **J.** Feet (Pedomancy)

17. **L.** Fire (Pyromancy)

18. **S.** Poop (Scatomancy)

19. **G.** Cheese (Tyromancy)

20. **A.** Actions of animals (Zoomancy)

The definition of "tyromancy" specifically calls for studying the coagulation of cheese. There have been medieval tales of people writing the names of suitors on cheeses and putting them in a cage with mice. Whoever's name is on the cheese the mice go for, that's your sweetheart for life. However, that might be closer to zoomancy (specifically "myomoancy" with mice and rats) rather than tyromancy.

KAREN

INTERLOPERS

BY CHRIS

Some synonyms are having a party—can you spot the party crashers? Below you'll find lists of four words each. Three are synonyms, meaning roughly the same thing. But one is distinctly different from the others, even though it's commonly confused with them. Maybe it's actually an antonym, maybe the meaning is sort of similar but has a significant difference, or maybe it's not related at all!

Can you find the interloper in each of these groups of words? (Bonus points if you know what it actually means!)

GROUPS OF WORDS

1. Unwilling, reluctant, reticent, disinclined

2. Lucky, fortuitous, charmed, fortunate

3. Bemused, nonplussed, unbothered, puzzled

4. Energize, enervate, vitalize, invigorate

5. Rowdy, boisterous, noisome, rambunctious

6. Tortuous, unpleasant, painful, disagreeable

7. Excess, plethora, abundance, surplus

8. Disaster, travesty, calamity, catastrophe

1. **Reticent**. It actually means "silent," while the others are variations of "unwilling."

2. **Fortuitous**. This means "occurring by coincidence or chance" and doesn't have the positive connotation of the other words.

3. **Unbothered**. The other words all mean "puzzled."

4. **Enervate**. While it might sound like "energize," this is an antonym of that and the other words—it means to sap energy.

5. **Noisome**. It means "smelly," not "loud."

6. **Tortuous**. This doesn't mean "torturous" or "painful," it means "twisty."

7. **Abundance**. All these words suggest a lot of something, but this is the only one that doesn't mean there's *too much* of something. Of course, "a bun dance" is what they do at bread weddings.

8. **Travesty**. Its meaning is "mockery" or "parody," not a "disaster."

ONE LETTER OFF

BY COLIN

A small change can make a big difference—and when it comes to changing words, you can't change much less than a single letter. For each question in this quiz I'll provide two clues, crossword-puzzle style. The answer will be a pair of words that are "one letter off" from each other.

Here's an example:

> **Clue: a.** *A common baked food*
> **b.** *A strong feeling of fear*

> **Answer:** *"bread" and "dread"*

The only difference between the two words is the "B" and the "D." In this case the different letter is at the beginning, but stay sharp—the answers may get a little tricky as you go along.

Got it? Good! Here we go…

CLUES

1. **a.** A brass orchestra instrument
   b. A Caribbean island nation

2. **a.** A large toothy predator
   b. A small rickety building

3. **a.** Something that burns intensely
   b. Something that cuts cleanly

4. **a.** A large flat fish
   b. A Japanese comic book

5. **a.** To lightly color
   b. To lightly burn

6. **a.** An original UK punk band
   b. An original DC Comics superhero

7. **a.** A type of dark beer
   b. A type of movie advertising

8. **a.** A household servant
   b. A military musician

1. "tuba" and "Cuba"

2. "shark" and "shack"

3. "blaze" and "blade"

4. "manta" and "manga"

5. "tinge" and "singe"

6. "(The) Clash" and "(The) Flash"

7. "porter" and "poster"

8. "butler" and "bugler"

JAPANESE WORDS YOU ALREADY KNOW

BY CHRIS

The English-language words we speak every day originated in many different languages, but as you might imagine, not a whole lot of them came from Japanese. But a few did, and not just the ones you might be thinking of right now.

Most Japanese words are made up of one or more *kanji* characters, each of which has a specific meaning. For example, *oru* means "fold," and *kami* means "paper," and you smoosh them together to get *origami*, the art of paper folding. I'll give you more of these meanings, and you tell me the English word that derived from Japanese. All of these are legal moves in an English-language game of Scrabble!

CLUES

1. Empty orchestra
2. Fire bowl
3. Whimsical picture
4. Divine wind
5. Strength car
6. Team leader
7. Harbor wave
8. Finger pressure
9. Sing dance skill
10. Pierced body
11. Art person
12. Wear-thing
13. Great lord
14. A little bit
15. Great wind

1. Karaoke (The Japanese pronunciation is closer to *car-ah-okay* than to *carry-okey*.)

2. Hibachi

3. Manga

4. Kamikaze

5. Rickshaw

6. Honcho (Yep, when you say "head honcho," you're speaking Japanese.)

7. Tsunami

8. Shiatsu

9. Kabuki

10. Sashimi (While there are theories, jury's out on why it's "pierced" and not "cut.")

11. Geisha

12. Kimono

13. Tycoon

14. Skosh (If someone says "Just a skosh," compliment them on their Japanese while you're pouring their drink.)

15. Typhoon

B-R-A-I-N Q-U-I-Z

BY CHRIS

This is the brainiest quiz in the book! Each of these definitions has a one-word answer, to be entered in the spaces provided. I've taken the liberty of filling in a few of the letters for you.

CLUES

1. Something deviating from the norm: __ B __ R __ A __ I __ N

2. A scraped knee, e.g.: __ B R A __ I __ N

3. Creative partnership: __ __ __ __ __ B __ R A __ I __ N

4. Surveillance: __ B __ __ R __ A __ I __ N

5. Uncivilized person: B __ R __ A __ I __ N

6. Shaking: __ __ B R A __ I __ N

7. Settlement of dispute: __ __ B __ __ R A __ I __ N

8. Deal: B __ R __ A I N

9. Former British prime minister: __ __ __ __ B __ R __ A I N

10. Political party: __ __ B __ R __ A __ I __ N

11. "E.g.," e.g.: __ B __ R __ __ __ A __ I __ N

12. Awe-inspiring: B R __ A __ __ __ __ __ I N __

1. ABERRATION (something deviating from the norm)

2. ABRASION (a scraped knee, e.g.)

3. COLLABORATION (creative partnership)

4. OBSERVATION (surveillance)

5. BARBARIAN (uncivilized person)

6. VIBRATION (shaking)

7. ARBITRATION (settlement of dispute)

8. BARGAIN (deal)

9. CHAMBERLAIN (former Prime Minister)

10. LIBERTARIAN (political party)

11. ABBREVIATION ("E.g.," e.g.)

12. BREATHTAKING (awe-inspiring)

ON YOUR MARKS
(OR HOW I LEARNED TO TELL A TILDE FROM A TITTLE)

BY COLIN

When you're a word nerd, you tend to run across a lot of funky characters; and I don't just mean your pub quiz teammates. So many of our best words come from other languages—or other eras—and with that comes a slew of interesting "diacritics," the special marks and modifications that transform otherwise normal letters and their pronunciation.

Below I've assembled an all-star lineup of diacritics, marks, accents, and even a veteran ligature to round things out. Some of these you likely know already, but with any luck you'll make a few new friends!

smörgåsbord

The small circle thing above the *a* is a **ring**—I know, hard to remember, right? It can appear above or below both vowels and consonants, signifying a "shifting" of the natural sound. (It's common in Swedish, so try counting the rings on your next trip to IKEA!)

señor

The little squiggly thing over the *n* is a **tilde**, and it indicates a /ny/ sound, as in "canyon." (In fact, canyon comes from the Spanish word *cañón*.) In the Spanish alphabet, *n* and ñ are considered separate characters (*ene* and *eñe*, respectively).

façade

The fancy tail thing on the bottom of the *c* is a **cedilla** (or cedille, after the French style). It signifies a *c* that sounds like an /s/ instead of a /k/, as in *garçon*. Today we use it primarily for French and Portuguese loanwords. The diacritic is a remnant of Old Spanish, where it originated as a hybrid *c/z* letter; over time the *z* shrank into a stubby tail shape beneath the *c* base. (*Ceda* is the Old Spanish word for *z*, so *cedilla* means "little z.")

München

The two dots over the *u* are an **umlaut**. Strictly speaking, "umlaut" refers to the process of sound modification—when a vowel shifts to take on a different sound—and not the mark itself; but nobody really enforces this distinction. (And though heavy metal band names with extraneous umlauts may look cool to English speakers, you can be assured it all appears quite silly to German speakers.)

coöperate

These *other* two dots over the second *o* are a **diaeresis**, also called a trema. Frequently confused with the umlaut mark, the diaeresis serves a different function: it signifies that a vowel should be pronounced independently from an adjacent vowel. For example, it makes clear that the *coop* in "cooperate" isn't pronounced like the *coop* in "chicken coop"; or that naïve isn't pronounced "nave." Most American publications have dropped the use of the diaeresis, but it still pops up in some pointedly old-fashioned outlets (we're looking at you, *New Yorker*).

shōgun

The flat bar thing above the *o* is a **macron**. The macron indicates a long vowel sound, like the *o* in "over." The name comes from *makro-*, the Greek root meaning "large" or "long."

ăpple

The curvy bowl-looking thing above the *a* is a **breve** mark. It signifies a short vowel sound, like the *o* in "otter." Think of the breve as the opposite of the macron.

hôtel

The upward-pointy thing above the *o* is a **circumflex** accent. In English the circumflex is mostly seen on French loanwords and phrases, like *fête* or *bête noire*, where it signifies a lengthened vowel sound or can stand in for a consonant. Words that become fully entrenched in English tend to lose the circumflex over time—*hôtel* becoming "hotel" is probably the best example of this.

Miloš

The downward-pointy thing above the *s* is a **caron**, also called a **háček**. This mark originated with modern Czech orthography (*háček* means "little hook" in Czech) and signifies a "palatalization" of the character below. So a č signifies a /ch/ sound, and a ž signifies /zh/. The origin of the word *caron* is mysterious—it doesn't appear in *Webster's* or in the *Oxford English Dictionary*—but it is generally preferred to háček in the field of typography.

juice

The little dot above a regular lowercase *i* or *j* is called a **tittle**. (And if you're anything like me, "tittle" makes you titter.) In its earliest sense, the word could apply to any mark above or below a letter; it comes from the same root as the word "title." Beyond the letters *i* and *j*, many Hebrew and Arabic letters also have tittles.

encyclopædia

Bonus! The proper name for this old-timey combined *a*/*e* letter is **ash** (sometimes styled æsh). This is an example of a ligature, two characters connected in a single "glyph" or symbol. It's sometimes found in older texts in words like *mediæval* and *archæology*, but these days it's usually rendered as *ae* (or simply *e*). Though not part of the English alphabet, it is used in several Nordic languages.

MY POLISH NAIL POLISH

BY DANA

A couple of months ago, I was looking at a bottle of nail polish and noticed that "polish" is pronounced differently from "Polish," as in a person from Poland. I immediately fell down an Internet research hole to find more magical words like this. Turns out that there are quite a few pairs of English words with the same spelling but different pronunciations and meanings. These special words are called "heteronyms" and "homographs."

Here's a different sort of crossword puzzle. Each entry in the grid has two definitions, which will lead you to heteronyms—spelled the same, but with different pronunciations.

ACROSS

2. **a.** A knot tied with two loops and two loose ends

    b. Bend the upper part of the body

5. **a.** Extremely small

    b. Sixty seconds

8. **a.** Not legally recognized

    b. Made weak or disabled by illness or injury

10. **a.** Express unwillingness to do

    b. Trash

12. **a.** Suitable or proper in the circumstances

    b. Take (something) for one's own use, typically without the owner's permission

14. **a.** Perceptible natural movement of air

    b. Move in a twisting or spiral course

16. **a.** Provide comfort from grief

    b. A control unit

17. **a.** Abandon

    b. Area with little rainfall

19. **a.** Evil, or morally wrong

    b. Absorbed by capillary action

DOWN

1. **a.** A small motorcycle

   b. To have been dejected and apathetic

3. **a.** Strike

   b. A sideboard meal

4. **a.** To be in charge or command of

   b. Chemical element with atomic number 82

6. **a.** An opening (such as a door, passage, or gate) that allows access to a place

   b. To fill (someone) with wonder and delight, holding their entire attention

7. **a.** Period of time at the end of the day

   b. Flattening, leveling, or smoothing

9. **a.** Moving or placing into a particular position

   b. Gently striking a golf ball

10. **a.** Farm machine that harvests and threshes

   b. To bring two or more things together

13. **a.** To act on or produce a change in

   b. Feign a certain characteristic

15. **a.** A type of bird

   b. Plunged steeply downward

18. **a.** Plant a seed

   b. Female pig

ACROSS

2. Bow
5. Minute
8. Invalid
10. Refuse
12. Appropriate
14. Wind
16. Console
17. Desert
19. Wicked

DOWN

1. Moped
3. Buffet
4. Lead
6. Entrance
7. Evening
9. Putting
11. Combine
13. Affect
15. Dove
18. Sow

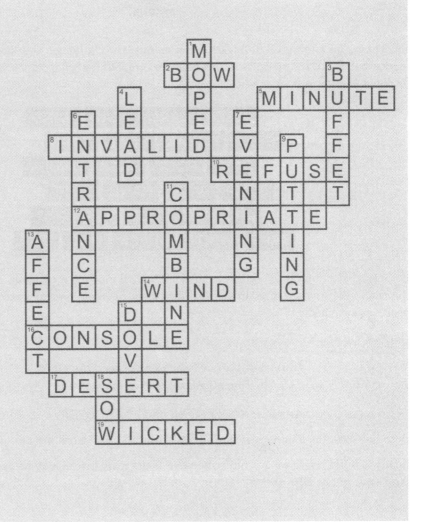

WORD SWAP

BY COLIN

I'm looking for a few good builders! If you're up to the challenge, check out the set of "word bricks" below. All the answers to this quiz are compound words, names, or phrases that can be made using words shown here.

For every question I'll provide two clues, and you'll give me a two-part answer. But here's the catch: both halves of your answer must use the same pair of word bricks, with their positions swapped.

Here's an example:

> **Clue: a.** *A party where friends spend the night*
> **b.** *To miss your alarm in the morning*

Answer: *SLEEPOVER and OVERSLEEP*

Both halves of the answer use the "SLEEP" and "OVER" word bricks—just swapped.

Ready to build? Here we go, and remember: some word bricks may be used more than once (and some not at all).

CLUES

1. **a.** A road that travels above another road
   b. A major Jewish holiday

2. **a.** Someone who never throws anything away
   b. A group of 1960s Las Vegas superstars

3. **a.** A brick-smashing game from the 1970s
   b. The sudden occurrence of a disease

4. **a.** A popular casino card game
   b. A popular comedic actor and musician

5. **a.** How you might describe a bouncy pop song
   b. How you might describe a junkyard car

6. **a.** A pro wrestling move
   b. A cartoon character from the 1990s

7. **a.** A flaky pastry
   b. To reverse a judicial decision

8. **a.** Something an orthodontist might give you
   b. A person who's really into cars

9. **a.** A scene filmed but not included in a movie
   b. Restaurant food you eat at home

10. **a.** The beginning of a pitcher's throw
    b. In the direction the breeze comes from

1. OVERPASS and PASSOVER

2. PACK RAT and RAT PACK

3. *BREAKOUT* and OUTBREAK

4. BLACKJACK and JACK BLACK

5. UPBEAT and BEAT-UP

6. HEADBUTT and BUTT-HEAD

7. TURNOVER and OVERTURN

8. HEADGEAR and GEARHEAD

9. OUTTAKE and TAKEOUT

10. WIND-UP and UPWIND (Yeah, the difference in pronunciation is a curveball, but I knew you could handle it.)

FANCY PANTS

BY DANA

Ms. Informed just received an invitation to a *very* exclusive party being thrown by some big name celebrities (think Diddy's annual White Party in the Hamptons, but less gauche). She's gotten her hands on a description of what everyone will be wearing, but unfortunately she has no idea what any of these things are. Help her out by drawing the items onto the figure below.

QUESTIONS

Draw the following apparel on the figure below.

1. Bateau line

2. Bolero

3. Boutonière

4. Cloche

5. Cravat

6. Epaulettes

7. Klompen

8. Knickerbockers

9. Peplum

10. Sunshade

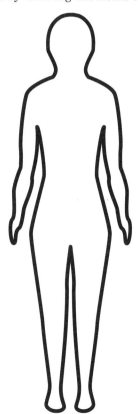

1. **Bateau line**: a neckline that curves from shoulder to shoulder.

2. **Bolero**: a short jacket, waist-length or shorter.

3. **Boutonnière**: a flower decoration worn on a jacket's lapel or in its lapel buttonhole.

4. **Cloche**: a bell-shaped hat that fits close to the head.

5. **Cravat:** a strip of fabric worn around the neck and tucked into an open shirt collar.

6. **Epaulettes**: a decorative shoulder piece, typically on the coat or jacket of a military uniform.

7. **Klompen**: Dutch wooden clogs.

8. **Knickerbockers**: short, baggy trousers that gather at the knee.

9. **Peplum**: a short overskirt attached at the waist to a jacket, blouse, or dress.

10. **Sunshade**: a parasol or umbrella.

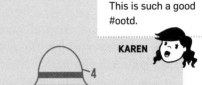

This is such a good #ootd.

KAREN

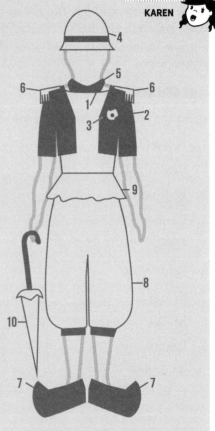

PARDON MY FRENCH

BY COLIN

As a confirmed linguistics nerd, I've always been fascinated by loanwords. In modern English we've taken more words from Latin than anywhere else; but of the "living" languages we've borrowed from, it's French that takes the cake. This quiz will test your knowledge of several French phrases firmly established as loanwords in English. While you may know what they *mean*, do you know what they literally translate to in French?

QUESTIONS

1. Introducing your boss by the wrong name isn't the end of the world, but it would certainly be considered a **faux pas**. What's the literal translation of faux pas?

2. Dessert menus in fancy restaurants often exhibit a French flair, tempting us with rich indulgences like **crème brûlée**. What's the literal translation of crème brûlée?

3. When you're doing something for the first time but are struck by a strong feeling of familiarity, you're experiencing **déjà vu**. What's the literal translation of déjà vu?

4. At the conclusion of an impressive stage illusion, a magician might exclaim "**Voilà!**" What's the literal translation of voilà?

5. Experimental artists and innovators are said to be part of the **avant-garde**. What's the literal translation of avant-garde?

6. A common material for children's arts and crafts is **papier mâché**, since it requires only simple ingredients: paper, water, and glue. What's the literal translation of papier mâché?

7. In suburban neighborhoods you'll frequently find dead-end streets, or **culs-de-sac**. What's the literal translation of cul-de-sac?

8. An increasingly popular way to prepare food is the **sous-vide** method, in which food in pouches is slowly cooked by heated water. What's the literal translation of sous-vide?

1. Faux pas translates as **"false step."** This is close in meaning to "misstep" in English, though *faux pas* technically implies a breach of social etiquette, not any general error or blunder.

2. Crème brûlée translates as **"burnt cream."** That sounds much more delicious in French, no?

3. Déjà vu translates as **"already seen."** (Déjà vu translates as "already seen.")

4. Voilà translates as **"look there."** If you accidentally confuse this word with "viola," at least be sure to pretend it was intentional.

5. Avant-garde translates as **"advance guard,"** in the sense that experimental or innovative people are in the front guard of cultural progress.

> I knew those seven years of French class would be good for *something*.
>
> **CHRIS**

6. Papier mâché translates as **"chewed paper."** And, yep… that's sure what it looks like.

7. Cul-de-sac translates as **"bottom of the sack,"** an allusion to a cul-de-sac's shape as seen from above. That said, it should be noted that in the same way "bottom" can mean "butt" or "ass" in English, *cul-de-sac* can also loosely translate to "ass of the sack." (I feel so dirty right now.)

8. Sous-vide translates as **"under vacuum,"** a reference to the vacuum-sealed pouches that hold the food during cooking.

WHO, WHAT, OR WHERE? PART II

BY COLIN

If you've ever taken a duffel bag full of bing cherries aboard a Ferris wheel, have I got just the quiz for you. (And afterward, I'd like you speak to a therapist.) In this installment of *Who, What, or Where?*, I've rounded up another batch of things-named-after-other-things, and your job is to tell me their namesakes. As always, remember that there's no shame in making up answers.

QUESTIONS

1. Who, what, or where is the **Ferris wheel** named after?

2. Who, what, or where is the **Geiger counter** named after?

3. Who, what, or where are **duffel bags** named after?

4. Who, what, or where is **Lyme disease** named after?

5. Who, what, or where is the **bing cherry** named after?

6. Who, what, or where is the **Uzi submachine gun** named after?

7. Who, what, or where are **Tiffany lamps** named after?

8. Who, what, or where is the **cardigan sweater** named after?

1. The Ferris wheel is named after **George Washington Gale Ferris, Jr.**, who designed his original ride for the 1893 World's Columbian Exposition in Chicago. (For this reason it's sometimes known as a "Chicago wheel.") Ferris envisioned a showcase attraction to rival the Eiffel Tower, centerpiece of the World's Fair in Paris four years earlier. And though his Ferris wheel was only one-quarter the height of the Eiffel Tower, it was undoubtedly a heck of a lot more fun.

2. The Geiger counter is named after **Hans Geiger**, a German physicist and professor who co-developed the radiation-detecting device in 1928, along with his PhD student Walther Müller.

3. Duffel bags are named after the **town of Duffel, Belgium**, where the heavy woolen fabric they were first made from originated. Today a duffel bag isn't necessarily made from wool, but it still connotes a simple, rugged, cylindrical bag favored by athletes, soldiers, etc.

4. Lyme disease is named after the **town of Lyme, Connecticut**, where there was an outbreak of the disease in 1975. The disease wasn't new, but due to its ability to "mimic" the symptoms of other illnesses, it went undiagnosed until scientists finally identified its cause (a bacterium transmitted via tick bites) in the 1980s.

5. Bing cherries are named after **Ah Bing**, a Chinese-born horticulturalist who emigrated to the U.S. in the 1850s. He worked for 35 years at the Lewelling family orchard in Milwaukie, Oregon, where the bing cherry cultivar was created in the 1870s.

6. The Uzi is named after **Uziel "Uzi" Gal**, a gun designer who created the instantly recognizable weapon for the Israeli Defense Forces in the late 1940s. Its compact size and impressive rate of fire has made it a staple of the Israeli army for more than 50 years. (It's also the weapon of choice for henchmen and mercenaries in countless cheesy action movies.)

7. Tiffany lamps are named after **Louis Comfort Tiffany**, whose influential New York glassworks studio began producing the lamps in the 1890s. The lamps that Tiffany and his team of artists created were prized for their Art Nouveau style and elegant stained-glass floral motifs. (Louis Comfort Tiffany is not to be confused with his father, Charles Lewis Tiffany, cofounder of the luxury jewelry firm Tiffany & Company.)

8. The cardigan is named after James Brudenell, the **7th Earl of Cardigan** and an officer in the British Army. In 1854, Brudenell famously led the Charge of the Light Brigade during the Crimean War, after which—despite the large number of casualties under his command—he received a hero's welcome back home in England. In a wave of "Cardigan mania" (a term I just invented), the distinctive button-up knit garment that he and his men wore as part of their field uniform caught on among civilians.

REMEMBERING THE BILL OF RIGHTS

BY CHRIS

We *always* get questions at pub quiz about the first 10 amendments to the U.S. Constitution, aka the Bill of Rights. Once we were told that there would be a question about the Bill of Rights during the Bay Area Grand Final, so I went looking for a good mnemonic to help us remember, once and for all, which amendment corresponds to which right, and...I found nothing.

Coming up goose egg on this one, I did what any of you would have done in the same situation: wrote my own poem about the Bill of Rights. And, dear reader, I will tell you this: we lost that Grand Final. But we got the question right! Now you can, too. Here's the poem, and what each line means.

Speech and such are the first rights.

Two: to arms, to arms! Let's fight!

Three's a crowd: you can't stay here.

Four, don't look through my things, dear.

Five will let you plead the fifth.

This is complemented with

Six, which says your day in court

Will be a speedy, public sort.

Lucky seven means a jury.

Eight means no cruel fates—don't worry.

We have nine lives and far more rights;

People and states have equal might.

Note that many of these amendments encompass a variety of rights; these are just the basics.

The First Amendment: protects the right to free speech, but also ("and such") the freedoms of association, religion, and the press.

The Second Amendment: protects the right to bear arms.

The Third Amendment: prevents the government from quartering soldiers in your house.

The Fourth Amendment: prevents unreasonable searches and seizures.

The Fifth Amendment: protects you from having to incriminate yourself in a trial—"pleading the fifth" means invoking this right to not answer a question.

The Sixth Amendment: guarantees the right to a speedy trial held in public.

The Seventh Amendment: guarantees you the right to a jury of your peers.

The Eighth Amendment: prohibits cruel and unusual punishment ("no big deal.")

The Ninth Amendment: says that the Constitution is not a definitive list of all of your rights, and that you might have other rights that aren't in there.

The Tenth Amendment: says that if a power hasn't been assigned to the federal government, then it belongs to the states or to the people.

THE *GOOD JOB, BRAIN!* CRYPTIC CROSSWORD

BY CHRIS AND SPECIAL GUEST PUZZLE-SETTER TYLER HINMAN

⟶≪∘≫⟵

I love cryptic crosswords, so much so that I really wanted to try my hand at making one. So we recruited our friend Tyler Hinman—puzzlemaker, *Good Job, Brain!* guest star, and five-time American Crossword Puzzle Tournament champion—to help create a *GJB*-themed cryptic especially for this book. (Thanks, Tyler!)

As for a regular crossword puzzle, you'll fill in the words suggested by the clues in the appropriate Across and Down columns. (Some of our favorite weird words are in here, so look out for those.) However, you may notice that these clues...make absolutely no sense. That's because unlike a regular crossword puzzle, the clues aren't just straightforward dictionary definitions—they're made up of various types of wordplay!

If you've never done a cryptic before, check out our Guide to Solving Cryptics on the following page before you start. There's definitely a learning curve to this kind of puzzle, but once you get the hang of it, it's a blast.

ACROSS

1. Cast metal...er, it's a natural flavoring (9)

6. Screw up Soseki novel, omitting its final two characters (5)

9. Rap with Eazy-E oddly follows start of "The Wire" (7)

10. Big mule rambling, "Actually, French fries were invented here" (7)

11. His gag, strangely, was "chieftain of puddings" (6)

12. Pal Billy runs to get program (8)

14. Which person sloshed in the middle to make a windy sound? (6)

15. Mexican painter primarily knew about hot lacquers, oils (5)

18. All set to hear singer Helen (5)

19. Newsman Donaldson on hosting a Polynesian (6)

22. Marvel hero's morbid bet (8)

24. Realist's losing it, going dotty for light beams (6)

26. Instantly send popular album to Egyptian chancellor (7)

27. Chopped audio recording conveys permission (7)

28. Smallish fraction of big top gets hot (5)

29. Cop's secret weapon is awesome drawings with music (5, 4)

DOWN

1. Like a good song, or like a good fielder? (6)

2. Unidentified bird slime ranges wildly (6)

3. Total upset: Oscar for "Horse Noise with Energy" actor Burrell (3–6)

4. Level unfinished, never going back (4)

5. Static caravan is moving target (6, 4)

6. Very good, like nonsense? (5)

7. Mr. Wheaton stuck in difficult time in the early evening (8)

8. Comedian I love's beginning to number a Broadway musical (8)

13. Put mouths on cake decorations—it's candy (10)

15. "Arable Oak" is confused, inaccurate, popular name for a marsupial (5, 4)

16. Nail hollow, outspoken thespian who's a sex symbol (4, 4)

17. Mommy, sweetie, is taking on rat race (8)

20. Busy animal's bedroom contains device for controlling rainwater (6)

21. Trapped in jailhouse, dupe is done for (4, 2)

23. Soft craving for tar (5)

25. Syndicate smuggling back hallucinogenic drug (4)

GUIDE TO SOLVING CRYPTICS

First note: cryptics are hard! Don't feel too bad if they at first seem very difficult. Try this puzzle, and if you like it, try some more. Eventually, the patterns will start to emerge in your brain. This is the first step in a long journey.

Each clue in this puzzle can be split cleanly into two halves: 1) the "straight" definition, which is the actual meaning of the word you're looking for, 2) and the "cryptic" definition, which gets you to the same answer via wordplay. You can always draw a single line somewhere within the clue and split it into these two halves.

The first trick is figuring out how to split it in two. It's often (intentionally) difficult to figure out where the dividing line between the two definitions should go—these clues are trying to trick you into thinking they're one single image or thought, whereas they're actually two different parts. Don't get bamboozled!

Once you think you know where the definition splits apart, you can use the "straight" definition and the "cryptic" definition together to figure out what word you're looking for. Remember: use both of them in tandem to find the right word. There might be many different words that fit the straight definition, but only one of them will match up with the wordplay.

Here's an example: "Slim monarch is cogitating (8)." The number in parentheses after the clue indicates the length of the final answer. (If the answer is a multiple-word phrase, you'll see the lengths of both words indicated and separated by a comma.)

In this case, the cryptic definition is "slim monarch," a synonym of THIN KING, which combines into THINKING. "Cogitating," the straight definition, is a synonym of "THINKING." This is an example of a **charades** clue, in which the target word is broken down into smaller segments.

(Note that sometimes, but not always, there might be a small word or two linking the two definitions together—in this example, it was "is.")

Anagrams: A favorite of everyone at *Good Job, Brain!*, anagrams are often used in cryptic clues. The letters to be anagrammed will be somewhere in the clue, and next to them will be a word indicating that you should anagram them. This will be a word suggesting movement or mixing things up. For example, the clue "Abby's crazy offspring (4)" has the indicator word "crazy." When you anagram "Abby" you get BABY, a word fitting the straight definition of "offspring."

Letter deletion: The clue may be asking you to take a word and remove some of its letters, either from the front, the back, or the middle. Similarly to anagrams, there will be an indicator word telling you what to do, such as "behead," "cut," "chop," "shorten," etc. But take note: unlike anagrams, these clues may not actually include the word from which you need to remove letters! For example, the clue "Behead leader of Dutch banking group (3)" has you delete a letter from "KING," a word that does not actually appear in the clue but is a synonym for "leader." You chop off the king's head K to get "ING," the Dutch financial corporation.

Hidden words: The answer might be right smack dab in the middle of the cryptic portion of the clue, but disguised. Maybe it's in the middle of a larger word, or it could be spanning two words. Again, an indicator word will let you know to look for something hidden, or being held by, the other words. For example, the clue "Flower planted in Dana's terrarium (5)" hints that the answer is "planted" inside the phrase. In this case, you can find "ASTER," a type of flower, in "Dana's terrarium."

Homophones: As you probably already know, these are words that sound the same but are spelled differently. In a clue, a homophone will be indicated by a word meaning "hearing," "talking," "audience," or anything else that has to do with words being said aloud. As with letter deletion, the homophone you're looking for probably won't be directly written in the clue. For example, the clue "Verbally slaughter Santa's ride (6)" hints at a homophone with "verbally." You can get "SLAY," a synonym of "slaughter," from its homophone "SLEIGH."

Containers: This is an indication that you should put one word inside of another word, or, to put it another way, that you should wrap one word around another. There will as usual be a word indicating that you should do this. For example, the clue "Internet joke about cereal was a barrier (8)," asks you to put another word for "Internet joke," a "MEME," around (that is, "about") another word for "cereal," "BRAN," to get MEMBRANE, which is a kind of "barrier."

Reversals: If you see a word meaning "goes backward" or "reverses," you might need to write a word (or part of a word) backward to get the answer. For example, the clue "Crazy shock, thrown backward (4)" tells you to take STUN, a synonym of "shock," and reverse its letters to get NUTS, meaning "crazy," the straight definition for this clue.

Double definitions: These clues, which can be as short as two words long, are simply two definitions of the answer, right next to each other. "Hold a big hairy animal (4)" might be "BEAR," a word meaning both "hold" (as a homonym) and "a big hairy animal."

Abbreviations: It's unlikely that a clue will revolve around only abbreviations, but often other types of clues will require you to abbreviate words or phrases that are commonly abbreviated when writing. For example, "north" can be N, "drive" can be D, "afternoon" can be PM, "time" can be T, "Republican" can be R, "male" can be M, and "bravo" can be B (in the NATO alphabet.)

All of the above: Particularly tricky cryptic clues might combine two or more of these types of wordplay! For example, if you saw "Brazilian currency dealer, confused, loses two notes (4)," you might start with the word "dealer," "lose" the musical "notes" D and E, and then anagram those "confused" letters to get REAL, the Brazilian currency.

If a clue seems tricky at first, don't give up—remember, this is a crossword! Move on, solve some other clues, and enter them into the grid. The letters that cross over the clues you're stuck on will be a big help toward finding the answer.

Here are the cryptic answers, using standard notation. If you want a more detailed explanation of how each one works (and to see where the clue is divided between the straight definition and the wordplay) see pages 234 to 238.

ACROSS

1. CAST + ORE + UM

6. BOTCH(an)

9. T + RAP + Eazy-E

10. BIG MULE anagram

11. HIS GAG anagram

12. PAL BILLY anagram

14. WHO + sloshed

15. Knew About Hot Lacquers, Oils

18. "Reddy" homophone

19. SAM + O(A)N

22. double definition

24. REALISTS anagram – IT

26. IM + HOT + EP

27. C(LEAVE)D

28. TENT + H

29. RAD + ART + RAP

DOWN

1. Double definition

2. RANGES anagram

3. O + NE(E)IGH + TY

4. NEVER – R reversed

5. MOBILE + HOME

6. Double definition

7. T(WIL)IGHT

8. HAM + I + L + TO + N

13. GOBS + TOPPERS

15. ARABLE OAK anagram

16. BRAD + "pit" homophone

17. MA + (RAT) + HON

20. B(EAVE)R

21. jailhoUSE DUPe

23. P + ITCH

25. synDICAte

1 C	A	2 S	T	3 O	R	4 E	U	5 M	■	6 B	O	7 T	C	8 H
A	■	N	■	N	■	V	■	O	■	U	■	W	■	A
9 T	R	A	P	E	Z	E	■	10 B	E	L	G	I	U	M
C	■	R	■	E	■	N	■	I	■	L	■	L	■	I
11 H	A	G	G	I	S	■	12 P	L	A	Y	B	I	L	L
Y	■	E	■	G	■	13 G	■	E	■	■	■	G	■	T
■	■	■	14 W	H	O	O	S	H	■	15 K	A	H	L	O
16 B	■	17 M	■	T	■	B	■	O	■	O	■	T	■	N
18 R	E	A	D	Y	■	19 S	A	M	O	A	N	■	■	■
A	■	R	■	■	■	T	■	E	■	L	■	20 B	■	21 U
22 D	E	A	D	23 P	O	O	L	■	24 L	A	S	E	R	S
P	■	T	■	I	■	P	■	25 A	■	B	■	A	■	E
26 I	M	H	O	T	E	P	■	27 C	L	E	A	V	E	D
T	■	O	■	C	■	E	■	I	■	A	■	E	■	U
28 T	E	N	T	H	■	29 R	A	D	A	R	T	R	A	P

ACROSS

1. **Cast metal...er, | it's a natural flavoring (9):** Take CAST straight from "cast," then add ORE, a synonym for "metal," and finish it off with UM, a synonym for "er." This gives you the "natural flavoring" CASTOREUM.

6. **Screw up | Soseki novel, omitting its final two characters (5):** If you take the classic Natsume "Soseki novel" *Botchan* and "omit" the "final two characters" in its name, you'll get BOTCH, a "screw up."

9. **Rap with Eazy-E oddly follows start of "The | Wire" (7):** Take RAP directly from "rap." If you then read the name "Eazy-E oddly," that is, read only the odd-numbered letters, you get EZE. The starting letter of "the" is T. Have RAP EZE "follow" the T to get TRAPEZE—a "wire."

10. **Big mule rambling, | "Actually, French fries were invented here" (7):** The letters of "big mule" are "rambling" all over to form the anagram BELGIUM, birthplace of fries.

11. **His gag, strangely, | was | "chieftain of puddings" (6):** The letters of "his gag" are "strange," or all mixed up. They move around to become the anagram HAGGIS, a dish known as the "chieftain of puddings."

12. **Pal Billy runs | to get | program (8):** The letters of "Pal Billy" are running around to form the anagram PLAYBILL, a type of "program."

14. **Which person sloshed in the middle | to make a windy sound? (6):** Start with "which person," a synonym of WHO. Then take the "middle" letters of "sloshed" to get OSH. Put them together to form the "windy sound" WHOOSH.

15. **Mexican painter | primarily knew about hot lacquers, oils (5):** If you take the "primary," or first, letters of the words "Knew About Hot Lacquers, Oils," you get KAHLO, the "Mexican painter."

18. **All set | to hear singer Helen (5):** "To hear" is an indicator that we're looking for a homophone. "Singer Helen" refers to Ms. Helen REDDY, a homophone of which is READY, meaning "all set."

19. **Newsman Donaldson on hosting a | Polynesian (6):** "Newsman Donaldson's" first name is SAM. "On hosting a" means that the word ON is "hosting," or contains, the letter A, which gives up the glyph OAN. Combine these parts to get SAMOAN, a certain sort of "Polynesian."

22. **Marvel hero | 's | morbid bet (8):** It's a double definition! A word that is both a "Marvel hero" and a "morbid bet" is DEADPOOL.

24. **Realist's losing it, going dotty | for | light beams (6):** The word "realist's" is "losing it"; that is, it's losing the letters I and T. Take those out and you get REALSS. Those letters then "go dotty"— that is, get all mixed up—to form LASERS, which are "light beams."

26. **Instantly send popular album | to | Egyptian chancellor (7):** "Instantly send" means the same thing as the abbreviation IM, instant message. Something "popular" is HOT. One type of "album" is an EP. Add all these up and you get IMHOTEP, an early "Egyptian chancellor."

27. **Chopped | audio recording conveys permission (7):** One type of "audio recording" is a CD, which "conveys" (that is, carries inside of it) LEAVE, a word meaning "permission." This gives up CLEAVED, a word meaning "chopped."

28. **Smallish fraction | of | big top gets hot (5):** A "big top" is a TENT. This becomes "hot," a word that can be abbreviated to H (check out the handles on your shower, for instance). Add the two parts and you get TENTH, a "smallish fraction."

29. **Cop's secret weapon | is | awesome drawings with music (5, 4):** "Awesome is a synonym of RAD. "Drawings" are a type of ART. RAP is a type of "music." Put them all together and you get a "cop's secret weapon," the RADAR TRAP.

DOWN

1. **Like a good song, | or |like a good fielder? (6):** This is a double definition, with the question mark indicating that the second definition is something of a pun (as in a standard crossword). A "good song" is CATCHY, and "a good outfielder" in baseball could be described as CATCHY, too.

2. **Unidentified bird slime | ranges wildly (6):** The letters in RANGES are arranged "wildly" to form *Good Job, Brain!*'s favorite word for mystery "bird slime"—SNARGE.

3. **Total upset: | Oscar for "Horse Noise with Energy" actor Burrell (3–6):** If you remember your NATO alphabet, "Oscar" should made you think of the letter O. A "horse noise" is a NEIGH, but it's "with energy," and energy is abbreviated as E, so we end up with ONEEIGH. Add actor Ty "Burrell" and you get ONE-EIGHTY—a total upset.

4. **Level | unfinished, never going back (4):** An "unfinished never"; that is, the word NEVER without its final letter, is NEVE. Since it's "going back" you should reverse it to EVEN—a word meaning "level."

5. **Static caravan | is | moving target (6, 4):** If you're from the UK, you might know that "static caravan" is a synonym for this clue's answer, MOBILE HOME. Otherwise, you could figure out this double definition from its cryptic part, since "moving" means MOBILE and "target" means HOME (as in homing missiles).

6. **Very good, | like nonsense? (5):** Again, if you're from the UK, you might know that BULLY is a synonym for "very good," and is also a punny answer to "like nonsense" (Bull-y).

7. **Mr. Wheaton stuck in difficult | time in the early evening (8):** "Mr. Wheaton" is surely actor WIL Wheaton. He's stuck in TIGHT, a word with the same meaning as "difficult." Stick the letters WIL into TIGHT and you get TWILIGHT, a time in the early evening.

8. **Comedian I love's beginning to number | a Broadway musical (8):** A "comedian" is also known as a HAM. Combine this with I, taken directly from "I." Add the "beginning" of the word "love's," an L. Then add TO, taken directly from "to." Finish with N, the abbreviation of "number." Put these all together and you get HAMILTON, the "Broadway musical" sensation.

13. **Put mouths on cake decoration— | it's candy (10):** This is bad advice, if you were to take it literally. Luckily, with cryptic clues we take almost nothing literally. A synonym for "mouths" is GOBS, and if we put them "on" a word meaning "cake decoration," or TOPPERS, we get GOBSTOPPERS, the everlasting Willy Wonka "candy."

15. **"Arable Oak" is confused, | inaccurate, popular name for a marsupial (5, 4):** The letters in ARABLE OAK are all "confused," or mixed up, anagramming to form KOALA BEAR. This is indeed an "inaccurate, popular name for" the "marsupials" in question; they're not really bears! They're marsupials!

16. **Nail hollow, outspoken | thespian who's a sex symbol (4, 4):** A BRAD is a type of "nail," and a "hollow" is another name for a PIT. When that's "outspoken," that is, when you say it out loud, it's a homophone of the sexy, sexy actor BRAD PITT.

17. **Mommy, sweetie, is taking on rat | race (8):** "Mommy" is often shortened to MA. "Sweetie" is a pet name, just like HON. When these two parts "take on" RAT in between them, they all form MARATHON.

20. **Busy animal | 's | bedroom contains device for controlling rainwater (6):** The word "bedroom" is often shortened to BR, and in this case it "contains" a "device for controlling rainwater," an EAVE. This gives us BEAVER, the "busiest animal" I know.

21. **Trapped in jailhouse, dupe | is | done for (4, 2):** Our answer is "trapped in" the phrase "jailhouse, dupe." Can you find it? It's USED UP, a phrase meaning "done for."

23. **Soft craving | for | tar (5):** If you read sheet music, you know that "soft" is often noted as P, for *piano*. (Yeah, this is tricky, but it comes up in a lot of cryptics, so remember it!) A "craving" for something is also known as an ITCH. These combine into PITCH, a kind of "tar."

25. **Syndicate smuggling back | hallucinogenic drug (4):** "Syndicate" is smuggling something, which means that our answer is contained somewhere within that word. But since it's smuggling it "back," you should look for a word running backward within "syndicate," like ACID, a "hallucinogenic drug."

THE *GOOD JOB, BRAIN!* GUIDE TO HOW TO PUB-QUIZ GOODER

BY THE WHOLE GANG

As we nerds continue our lifelong quest to take over the world, one unsuspecting bar at a time, pub trivia has been gaining a whole lot of popularity. Even you might be wondering: how can I, too, do pub trivia?

The solution may be as simple as heading over to your local watering hole, grabbing a pencil, and start answering questions! Note that it would be helpful if someone is actually administering a pub quiz on the night that you do this.

As this book goes to press, the *GJB* crew has been playing pub trivia together for eight years. Over those years, we've developed some rules of thumb that have helped us achieve victory, or at least learn something when we go down in defeat.

Here's the best advice we've got:

HAVE FUN

(Not too much fun.) Nobody's going to get rich and famous doing pub trivia. The top prize is probably a pitcher or two of beer. Relax and enjoy yourselves. Have a drink, if you want—it's a pub! But don't be that person who gets hammered at trivia, either. You're here because you enjoy competition. (So make sure, at the end of the day, that you're *enjoying* it.)

KNOW YOUR QUIZ

All pub quizzes are not created equal! Try a few different venues if you have options, and see which you like the best. Some quiz hosts hate it when you point out that they've made an error; some are fine with that. Some quiz hosts love trick questions; some never do trick questions.

Shop around for a trivia host that fits your desires. But more than that, once you know what types of questions your host does or doesn't ask, you should get a leg up on figuring out the answers. Over time we've learned the average difficulty of the questions at our bar, which means we can rule out answers that would make the question too easy or too hard.

FIND A SPORTS PERSON

Of course, it's best to build a team of friends you'd like to hang around and spend more time with, because as we've said, the point is to have fun! But sports questions come up a lot in traditional pub trivia, and not having a sports person on your team will put you at a significant competitive disadvantage. The only zero our team ever got on a trivia round was when Chris and Karen had to do a sports round by themselves. We're lucky that Karen's sports-loving coworker Colin joined the team shortly after, because since then he's single-handedly won us at least three or four points a night on sports alone.

Of course, as trivia has become a more popular pastime, subject-specific trivia nights have also been popping up. So you might be able to find a way to play pub trivia without ever being asked about a single batting average! (Of course, if you've got sports on lockdown but miss a lot of pop culture questions, you may also need to fill in those knowledge holes with more diverse quizzers.)

READ THE NEWS, LISTEN TO MUSIC

At least a passing familiarity with the latest news stories and the top *Billboard* hits will go a long way—if your particular trivia host cares about this, of course. Get to know what kind of music your quiz host likes. It will show up a disproportionate amount of the time!

DON'T CENSOR YOURSELF

Anything that jumps into your head as a possible answer is worth saying out loud. Anything worth saying out loud is worth saying out loud twice, to make sure that your other team members actually *heard* you over the clattering of silverware, the clinking of pints, and the never-ending noises in their own heads.

Memory, and the way we connect dots and remember things, is weird. Your answer might be wrong—it might be *really* wrong—but merely by virtue of you saying it, you might jog someone else's memory: "Oh, it's not Three Dog Night, but it *is* Cat Stevens." Say everything that comes to mind.

Corollary I: Don't Be Mr. or Ms. "I SAID THAT!" One of our running jokes at pub quiz is that once a night, we'll hear someone on another team scream "I SAID THAT!" This usually happens right after the quizmaster reads out an answer, the implication being that the team didn't write down the correct answer, even though their teammate threw it out there as a possibility.

Let's break this down. In our experience, it's likely that for many if not most questions you get wrong, someone will have said the right answer at some point during the discussion. You might have "said it," but when you said it, was it just one entry in a stream-of-consciousness rundown of a dozen possible answers? If so, why would your team have picked that answer over another?

If you were, indeed, overruled by your team even though you fought hard for the right answer, trust us—your team doesn't need reminding that they didn't listen to you. (And neither does the rest of the bar, if we're being honest.)

Corollary II: Don't censor other people. For more points, *and* for the sake of your friendships, try to foster an environment in which everyone feels comfortable saying whatever comes to mind. If you're stuck, try asking a silent teammate what they're thinking.

This is the magic of pub trivia: a team can arrive at correct answers that the same people, working independently, could not. You are more than the sum of your parts, but only if you work as a team.

LEARN THE DIFFERENCE BETWEEN KNOWING YOU ARE RIGHT AND THINKING YOU ARE RIGHT

This can be the hardest lesson to learn, because it only comes with experience—which means messing up real bad first.

At some point, you will absolutely believe that you have the correct answer—no question, would bet a thousand dollars on it, will make a big show of talking your teammates out of their (actually right) answer. And you'll be wrong. Complete and total egg-on-face disaster. Maybe you'll even lose first place that night by a single point.

Don't feel bad if this sounds painfully familiar—we've all been there. Our brains hold a ton of useful trivia, but they can also persuade us we're right even when we're not. Playing pub trivia over a long span of time means learning to recognize this in yourself, and to truly be able to tell the difference between "I am right" and "I think I might be right."

When we're playing together, our shorthand for this is "100 percent," "99 percent," and "Maybe." And after eight years of playing together, we've learned (after some hard lessons) when "100 percent" actually means 100 percent: this is something we truly, definitely know for sure. Like asking Colin what Michael Jordan's jersey number was,[31] or asking Chris what games were originally packed in with the Nintendo Entertainment System.[32]

But if we think we're right but admit to ourselves that we're not *sure*, it's "99 percent." That's a signal that our team should really look at this answer, but we should try our best to poke holes in it or come up with alternatives. But 99 percent is more than just a guess. It's "Hey guys, I really think this is it."

"Maybe" is anything lower than 99 percent. You're just throwing something out there that sounds good, for the team to chew on. You're not married to it, and you won't be mad if it turns out to be the right answer after passing on it.

Talk about your reasoning. If you're not totally sure about a suggested answer, tell your team how you got there. Talking through your process may elicit confirmation from your teammates that you're on the right track—or it may expose flaws in your reasoning that will eliminate a wrong answer.

DISCUSS GUESSES BEFORE WRITING DOWN AN ANSWER

Sometimes your quiz host will hand out a sheet for you to fill in. For example, at our local quiz we often have to label photos of famous people, or match up cities with airport names, etc. If your team is like most, you'll pass the page around and each person will fill in some answers. (In a dark bar, this may be the only way to make sure everyone gets a close look.)

---

31. 23...then 45...and then 23 again. Oh, and 12 for a single game.
32. *Duck Hunt* and *Gyromite*. (Nope, it wasn't *Super Mario Bros.*)

GOOD JOB, BRAIN!

In this case, it is *poison* to write down an answer that you're not 100 percent sure of. Even if you're "just guessing," you're priming your other team members to see what you see.

For example, if you write "Anna Kournikova" under a photograph of Chloë Grace Moretz and pass it to the other team members, it's quite possible that they'll scan the page, see the name and the person, and think, "Oh, right, Anna Kournikova"—*even if they would have correctly identified Chloë Grace Moretz had the answer line been blank*. Don't even write your guess to the side, or lightly pencil it in, or anything. Let your teammates see the page with fresh eyes.

The best way to handle a picture round is to pass it around, let each team member fill in only what they are 100 percent sure about, and then come together as a group to discuss the answers you have to guess at.

KEEP TRACK OF YOUR OWN SCORE

Trivia hosts are under a lot of time pressure, trying to grade a bunch of quiz sheets under dim lighting at a cramped table in a noisy barroom. We've found that missing points for correct questions is a *regular* occurrence. When the host reads out the answers for each round, keep meticulous track of each question you answered correctly, and tally up your own score. If there's a discrepancy (a good pub quiz host will update everyone on the point standings at the end of each round), go up and ask about it. Note that you should ask as soon as there is a discrepancy, so you can narrow it down to the exact round that was a problem.

DO NOT: March up to the host and say, "You're wrong, Wrongy McWrongerson! Correct your stupid mistake!" or any variation on same. This will not endear you to the host or the facility. Also, you'll look like a tremendous drunken fool if you are in error.

DO: Walk up during the between-rounds break and say, "Hey, we think we had nine questions right on that round, but we only got eight points. Can you show us the paper?" At this point, a good trivia host will find your sheet and go over it again with you. (If your trivia host bristles at the mere suggestion that there might have been an error and refuses to consider it, find a new venue.)

DO NOT: Bother with any of this if the discrepancy was in the final round and you won first place anyway and the point doesn't matter. Pick your battles.

POLITELY POINT OUT QUESTION ERRORS

Let's say that the host misidentifies Paul McCartney's "Wonderful Christmastime" as a Beatles song and won't accept McCartney as an answer. Here (again, *if the point matters*) you should politely point this out, maybe using some additional documentation on your smartphone. Hopefully some other teams will join in with you on this. In this case, it's polite to simply accept the trivia host's word as final—a little bit of pushing is fine, but don't go any further than a polite inquiry. You don't want to jam up the proceedings for everyone else. The host may be working for a larger company and may not even have the power to change the answers. (If this keeps happening, find a new venue.)

STUDY

The Periodic Table of Elements? The Oscars? The amendments to the U.S. Constitution? There are many big, broad topics like this that trivia masters love, and all it takes to study them are an Internet connection or a library card. Morning commutes are great times to sneak in some extra studying on your smartphone! (Alternatively, record a weekly trivia podcast for four years.)

LOOK FOR PATTERNS

Trivia quiz writers are human, and it's possible that they pulled from similar sources or had the same things on their mind when they wrote the questions for a round, or for a quiz. If Marlon Brando showed up in the picture round, maybe the answer to that movie question in the next round is *The Godfather*. Now, we don't use this to *come up* with answers, but we use it to *break ties* if we need to write something down but can't decide.

LEARN TO SETTLE DISPUTES

It's going to happen at some point: two or more members of your team will come to loggerheads over an answer, and you'll need to settle it. Yelling "I think I'm right!" until one person caves is not the healthiest way to solve things, so here's the system we use: give each feuding team member a scrap of paper and have each of them write down a number from 1 to 10.

This number does **not** indicate *how sure are you that you're right:* rather, it indicates *how upset you will be if we don't use your answer and it turns out you were right.* The person with the higher number wins. This avoids fighting over who's more confident in an answer and focuses on who cares the most. This works for us a surprising amount of the time! It also stops us from getting too mad.

If you really, well and truly, cannot find a way to decide between two answers, just flip a damn coin. If you have more than two potential answers, write them down on scraps of paper, crumple them, shake them up in your hands, and let only one fall out. That is your answer, delivered to you by the Fates. The Fates are never wrong. (If the Fates are wrong, see previous sentence.)

When you're asked to give a number as an answer and you have no idea, "three" is a good bet.

HAVE FUN

Seriously, though.

GOOD JOB, BRAIN! THANKS

First and foremost, our lovable listeners (from Louisiana to Luxembourg), who legitimately live on a legendary level; whose laughter and loyalty we are lucky to have in our loony lives.

Thanks to our great friend Rob Sable, former Baby Dog Time member and Lobetrotter #1, for his constant support. Thanks to Liam, Mark, and everyone at Brainstormer for bringing us together originally; No Reservations and Party of Five for the competition; our good luck charm, Ian; Jake Hadary, our quiz finals ringer; and Andy, Jonathan, and everyone else who's subbed in for trivia competitions. You've all taught us a lot (and won us some clutch points)! Ryan Scott and the Geekbox crew did a lot to help us get started in the podcast world. Thanks to our special guest puzzlemasters Tyler Hinman and Neville Fogarty. More thanks to Andrew Yang (who drew our iconic beaver mascot), Courtney Patubo Kranzke, Derek Ku, and Rob Walch. Still more thanks to Shannon Prickett for inspiring us with lunchtime trivia sessions. We can't thank every *Good Job, Brain!* fan by name, so we'll just thank Madeline Stein for her very early, unflagging, and encouraging support of this endeavor. And, of course, our eternal gratitude to the 100 Kickstarter backers who helped us get off the ground!

And thanks to Otis, the original Baby Dog, our team mascot and the most loyal friend anybody ever had.

KAREN

Thanks to PJ, and my family of humans and animals. But a shout-out to my mom, who tricked me into thinking that learning was fun by giving me an old-school LED arithmetic question machine when I was four and telling me it was a video game.

COLIN

Thanks to my family; Pixie and Mei Mei (the Pod-cats); and my amazing wife, Betty, whose constant support makes me better and helps make *Good Job, Brain!* great.

DANA

Thanks to my family, especially Harmony, who helped me sketch Liberace; Hunden, who forced me to go outside at least twice a day; and Erik, who is always happy to listen to my "cool" stories.

CHRIS

Thanks to my wonderful and patient wife, Regina, and our son, Chris, who let me record podcasts and write books on the weekends, and all the great teachers I've had in my life (too many to list)! Also Ricky, occasional Pod-dog.

ABOUT *GOOD JOB, BRAIN!*

First launched via Kickstarter in 2012, *Good Job, Brain!* is a weekly-ish podcast devoted to all things trivial. It won the Stitcher Award for Best Games and Hobbies Show in 2013, was named one of *The Guardian*'s top 10 podcasts for road trips, and is hosted by a real live pub trivia team, who love animals, Laffy Taffy jokes, and hiding puzzles on book covers.

ABOUT THE AUTHORS

Karen Chu: a designer at Twitch, brews mead, runs marathons in costume, and is way into vexillology.

Colin Felton: a designer and Web developer, collects an unhealthy amount of *Star Wars* droids.

Dana Nelson: a prolific game designer, is a word nerd and pop culture enthusiast, and not Belgian.

Chris Kohler: games editor at *Wired*, collects video games and is the author of *Power-Up: How Japanese Video Games Gave the World an Extra Life.*